The
Creative
Breakfast

The
Creative
Breakfast

Simple, Nutritious, Delicious Recipes
for the Most Important Meal of the Day

Ellen Klavan

HPBOOKS

HPBooks
Published by The Berkley Publishing Group
A member of Penguin Putnam Inc.
200 Madison Avenue
New York, NY   10016

First edition: April 1998

Published simultaneously in Canada.

The Penguin Putnam Inc. World Wide Web site address is
http://www.penguinputnam.com

Library of Congress Cataloging-in-Publication Data
Klavan, Ellen.
    The creative breakfast : simple, nutritious, delicious recipes for
the most important meal of the day / Ellen Klavan. — 1st ed.
        p. cm.
    ISBN 1-55788-284-3
    1. Breakfasts. I. Title.
TX733.K58   1998
641.5'2—dc21   97-16870
                                                                                        CIP

Printed in the United States of America

10 9 8 7 6 5 4 3 2 1

For Spencer

Contents

Acknowledgments

Thanks, first and foremost, to my family and friends, who cheerfully (for the most part) ate breakfast three times a day, especially during the summer of 1996, and provided equal measures of encouragement and constructive criticism.

Thanks to Aileen Libassi and Roderick Huntress, professional chef and inspired amateur respectively, for their culinary and literary input, to Susan Clemente for research assistance beyond the call of duty, and to Mary Ousley and Chris Niles for unparalleled moral support. My agent, Kris Dahl, and my editor, Jeanette Egan, have been wonderful. Thanks, too, to Irene Prokop and John Duff at Penguin Putnam. Thanks as ever to my husband, Andrew Klavan, for his forbearance, sense of humor and gracious editorial assistance.

Introduction

What's for Breakfast?

The ancient warrior Ulysses began his day with bread soaked in wine. The Romans breakfasted lightly on bread and cheese or dried fruits. Feudal lords in medieval castles served meat, fish, eggs, and more at the morning meal—the precursor of the full English breakfast of bacon, sausage, pudding, kippers, poached eggs, toast, and, of course, lashings of tea.

Here in America, tastes in breakfast are constantly changing. At times we have splurged on the "farmer's breakfast" of steak and eggs, pancakes and maple syrup, with coffeecake on the side. At other times we have reined ourselves in with the "health-food" breakfast of grains and juices, first introduced by Protestant preachers in the nineteenth century. Both breakfasts have gone in and out of style.

Even in the past few decades, American tastes and ideals of good health have vacillated wildly, so that the breakfasts you ate as a child may be very different from those you eat now. My friend Suzanne, for instance, recalls the breakfasts her mother served in the 1950s: hot oatmeal swimming in fresh dairy cream, bacon and eggs, pancakes slathered with butter, and maple syrup. These weren't special Sunday breakfasts; Suzanne sat down to this kind of meal every morning of the week.

Sounds great, doesn't it? But that was before the new era of nutritionists spoiled the fun by telling us we had to cut back on fat, boost our fiber intake, and replace simple sugars with complex carbohydrates if we wanted to live long enough to meet our grandchildren. Happily, there are plenty of delicious breakfast foods that meet the nutritionists' new criteria.

The breakfasts Suzanne serves her own family are far more nutritious and, to my mind, even more inviting than the ones she ate as a child. Fresh fruit dominates the menu—cantaloupe with a dollop of low-fat yogurt is a favorite—while whole-grain cereals, bagels, and other breads make up the balance of the meal. Pancakes or waffles topped with fresh fruit are popular, too. Eggs and bacon aren't unknown to her breakfast table, but they're served rarely and in moderation.

In fact, moderation is the keynote of the new approach to breakfast. You can have all the breakfast foods you love, providing you don't overdo it. One poached egg served in a basket of spinach on a slice of tomato, for example (see page 106), is a tasty and filling alternative to a three-egg omelette. French toast served with fresh fruit instead of maple syrup is another satisfying compromise. And creative use of low-fat dairy substitutes will turn cholesterol nightmares into high-fiber dream foods.

Is Breakfast Necessary?

Your mother told you not to skip it. If you have kids, you probably tell them to eat it. But are you really convinced that breakfast matters? If you haven't got time to eat first thing in the morning, can't you just make up for the missing calories at lunch? Isn't skipping breakfast, when you're not really all that hungry, a good way to lose weight? The answer, according to nutritionists, is a resounding *no!*

During sleep your metabolism slows down so that you're able to make it through to morning without waking up in the middle of the night hungry. Nevertheless, by the time dawn rolls around, your body's ready energy supplies are depleted. If you don't replenish your energy banks, your body will turn to its reserve supply, feeding on fat and other stored energy. The problem with this is that the work involved in using stored energy is taxing and it can leave you feeling light-headed and weak. Your concentration may be less focused and your mental processes in general less acute. So, if you have a big meeting tomorrow morning and you need your wits about you, eat your breakfast, just like your mother always told you. Likewise if you're taking an exam, running in a marathon, or chasing after small children all day, eat before you get going.

Now, if you're dieting you probably have found that little remark about the body feeding on its own fat pretty attractive. Granted, healthy weight loss occurs when food intake is reduced and excess weight reserves are drawn upon to sustain energy. However, skipping breakfast is acknowledged by all responsible weight-loss programs to be one of the seven deadly sins of dieting.

In the first place, responsible dieting—the kind that works and lasts—depends on a program of carefully planned meals eaten throughout the day. Perhaps more compelling (if you only have two months to fit into your favorite suit for your daughter's wedding): *skipping breakfast doesn't work.*

If you skip breakfast, hunger is likely to drive you to grab the nearest source of nourishment (a candy bar, for instance) in the middle of the day. You're liable to be so hungry at lunchtime that you "allow" yourself to consume even more calories than you would have had you eaten reasonable portions of both meals. In short, by missing breakfast, you may be letting yourself in for weight gain, not loss.

Several recent studies have found that people who don't eat breakfast tend to have higher cholesterol levels and to be more overweight than those who do eat breakfast. One reason for this is that healthy breakfast foods like cereals and fruits tend to be lower in fat and cholesterol than the processed foods you're likely to eat throughout the day.

Another reason breakfast eaters are healthier is that research defends that old adage that "three meals a day"—or more!—is the best way to eat. The body burns smaller amounts of calories more efficiently than larger ones. So you'll get more benefit from the nutrients in the foods you eat if you spread them out over the day and you'll also lose weight faster if you're reducing overall calories.

In some ways, our American eating pattern, which often begins with a small breakfast and culminates in a big evening meal, makes very little nutritional sense. In the morning, we have a day's work ahead of us, whereas at night we are bound for the undemanding task of sleep. It's hard to change the habits of a lifetime but it's worth considering rearranging your routine to eat a bigger breakfast and a lighter dinner.

One final case for the morning meal. If you have a family, eating breakfast is an important social occasion. With our hectic schedules, it may be the only time when the whole family sits down together. As time goes on—when children become busy teenagers with evening pursuits of their own, for instance—finding time to be together as a family can become more difficult. Setting a pattern of breakfasting together now can ensure that at least once a day everyone is gathered together around the table.

A Healthy Breakfast

Okay, so I've talked you into eating breakfast. What kind of breakfast should you be eating? Like the other meals you eat, breakfast should contain a little of everything—some fruits and vegetables if you're in the mood, grain-based foods, dairy products like milk or yogurt, or some other good sources of calcium.

Ideally, the foods you eat for breakfast will release their energy slowly so that your blood-sugar levels will remain more or less constant throughout the morning. High-fiber foods like oatmeal and fresh fruit release their energy slowly, as do low-fat dairy products. Foods that raise your blood sugar rapidly—white bread, for instance, as well as orange juice and jam—give you an immediate surge of energy but then let you down rapidly as your blood sugar drops.

Here are some general points to keep in mind as you plan your meals.

Fat   The F-word! Fat has gotten such a bad name lately I'm sure it would be held responsible if our country went to war. Heart disease, obesity, cancer, and a host of other ailments have been linked—correctly—to excess dietary fat. However, for all the bad press it's been getting, it's important to bear in mind that fat is not all bad. The body needs some fat to survive and in general food needs some fat to taste good.

The American Dietetic Association recommends that you keep the fat content of your diet below 30 percent of your total calories. Of that 30 percent no more than 10 percent (that is, one third of the 30 percent) should come from saturated fat. At first glance, 30 percent looks like a lot and you may be thinking, "Great! I can have bacon and sausage with my eggs tomorrow morning!" Sorry to let you down, but you need to bear in mind the caloric density of fat: one tablespoon of butter contains 108 calories, as compared to 87 in a medium apple or a slender 14 in a cup of chopped spinach.

Exploring the fat question more deeply, there are, according to nutritionists, "good" fats and "bad" fats," in particular those that are unsaturated (good) versus those that are saturated (bad). As a rule, animal fats like lard and butter are less healthy than vegetable oils, so try to favor the latter.

While we're on the subject of fat (and breakfast), it's a good time to raise the question of butter versus margarine. Butter is on the "bad" list because it is a saturated fat. But margarine contains trans–fatty acids, which may be just as bad or worse for you. (The research on margarine is far from complete.) While nutritionists battle out this question, you can bypass the problem by using unsaturated vegetable oil wherever possible. But don't check into the Mayo Clinic if you have a small pat of butter on your morning toast.

Cholesterol   Like its counterpart, fat, cholesterol is bad for you in excess but good for you in moderation. As you probably know, cholesterol is only found in animal products, including not only meat but also eggs, milk, and other dairy products. The lower the fat content of a milk product, the lower its cholesterol content as well, so you can't go too far wrong with your cardiologist by drinking skim milk and eating nonfat yogurt. The American Dietetic Association recommends limiting our cholesterol intake to an average of about 300 milligrams a day.

The big cholesterol stumbling block, especially for breakfast lovers, is eggs. What's breakfast without eggs, after all? It's hard enough to give up old standards like eggs-over-easy and scrambled eggs. It's harder still to contemplate giving up breakfast favorites like pancakes, French toast, and muffins, all of which usually contain some egg. But the yolk of a large egg is one of the most concentrated sources of cholesterol you can find—213 milligrams (and about 5 grams saturated fat).

Happily, there are creative ways to combat cholesterol without giving up eggs completely. Two cholesterol-free egg whites are roughly the culinary equivalent of a whole egg and can be used in many recipes that call for an egg. In many recipes, you won't even notice the absence of the egg yolk and in others you can play around, for instance, by using one whole egg and two egg whites in a recipe that calls for two eggs.

Sugar   Whether it's white or brown, granulated or soft, sugar is sugar. So, for all intents and purposes, are honey, maple syrup, and molasses. With minor variations, the nutritional value of sweeteners is zero to negligible (except for the calories). Apart from tooth decay, sugar is often held responsible for obesity, although this may not be completely fair to sugar, since most of the sweet foods that we crave also contain a lot of fat. Many doctors say that while sugar isn't especially good for you, it's not particularly bad for you either. A few doctors and many dietitians and other health professionals believe that sugar may be responsible for mood swings and that it contributes to a variety of chronic health problems. On the plus side, sugar, like fat, makes food taste better. It makes sense to cut back on sweeteners without completely giving up the good-tasting food your family loves. Providing plenty of fruit at breakfast is a good way of satisfying everyone's sweet tooth without overloading on processed sugar.

Fiber   So much for the bad guys. Here's something that's good to eat for breakfast. Fiber, which is found abundantly in grains, fruits, and vegetables, comes in two forms, soluble and insoluble. The American Dietetic Association recommends that you consume about 20 to 35 grams of fiber (a combination of soluble and insoluble) daily.

Soluble fiber is the nutritional superhero of the day because it can actually lower cholesterol in the blood. That's why you hear so much good press about foods like oatmeal.

Insoluble fiber is the indigestible part of plant foods. (Other terms used over the years include *bulk* and *roughage*.) Without going into vulgar detail, let me point out that insoluble fiber, which passes relatively quickly through the system, can help prevent constipation and is generally considered to be beneficial to the digestive system, even so far as warding off colon cancer and other serious health risks. (Soluble fiber is an aid to digestion too.) Another key benefit of insoluble fiber is that you can eat a lot of it without putting on weight.

It's easy to include fiber because so many high-fiber foods—fresh fruit and whole-grain breads and cereals, for example—are naturals for breakfast. It's easy too, to add fiber to your other breakfast choices by choosing a high-fiber cereal or by using whole-wheat flour and adding wheat bran when baking.

Protein   Nutritionists agree that Americans eat far more protein than they need or than is good for them. The American Dietetic Association recommends that you derive 10 to 20 percent of your calories from protein. That percentage can easily be met by a small amount of meat or just as easily by vegetarian foods. Milk and all its derivatives are protein rich. Since we're accustomed to eating meat at lunch and dinner, I think breakfast is a good time to cut back. You'll find small amounts of meat in some of the recipes in this book but most contain no meat.

Carbohydrates   The majority of the foods you eat (about 50 to 60 percent of your calorie intake) should be carbohydrates, also known as sugars and starches. Many high-fiber foods, like fruit and whole-grain bread, are carbohydrates. Try to emphasize complex carbohydrates (like whole-grain breads and cereals) over simple carbohydrates (like sugar).

The encouraging fact is that with a little common sense it's quite easy to make a delicious breakfast that meets your nutritional needs. A bowl of high-fiber cereal with low-fat milk and a glass of orange juice; fruit salad with yogurt and an oatmeal scone; whole-grain pancakes with strawberry-maple sauce and a frothy fruit drink—any one of these can make a satisfying and healthy start to your day.

A Creative Breakfast

A creative breakfast is one that tastes great while meeting your nutritional requirements. It's low in fat and cholesterol without necessarily being fat free. By the same token, sugar is kept to a reasonable minimum.

The recipes in this book come from several sources. First, innkeepers and bed-and-breakfast owners around the country sent me their most popular recipes, which I tested and sometimes modified to bring down the fat and sugar content. Next, friends and family members gave me their favorite recipes. Finally, I adapted classic breakfast recipes to meet contemporary nutritional standards.

Please consult the following section, "A Word About Ingredients." You'll find that I define an egg, for instance, as either a whole egg, two egg whites, or equivalent commercial egg substitute. Milk can be whole, low-fat, or skim, and so on.

The words *test kitchen* always conjure up in my mind a large immaculate space with gleaming work surfaces, highly polished copper pots and pans, and neatly stacked mixing bowls. Through this space, serene white-clad chefs sail patiently through the motions of preparing precisely measured meals.

Nothing could be further from an accurate description of my kitchen, which is a crowded, bustling space where children help make my recipes, my husband sticks his fingers in the batter and tastes the muffins before they've cooled properly, and guests wander through making suggestions as they pour themselves countless cups of coffee.

Most of us don't have time to prepare elaborate gourmet meals at any time of the day, far less first thing in the morning. These recipes have worked for me, over and over again, because they're simple and easy to follow even in the midst of chaos. I hope you'll enjoy them as much as I have.

A Word About Ingredients

Unless otherwise indicated, the recipes in this book are flexible enough to use a range of ingredients, like skim or whole milk, for example, and nonfat or full-fat yogurt. Which ingredients you use will depend on your diet and health concerns as well as your family's tastes.

Obviously, you can't make eggs sunny side up without using whole eggs, so when a whole egg—or full-fat milk—is required, I'll let you know. Otherwise I define ingredients as follows:

Eggs   You may use a whole egg, two egg whites, or a commercial liquid egg substitute that dresses up egg whites so they look more like whole eggs. You may also choose to reduce the number of yolks by using, for instance, one whole egg and two egg whites for "two eggs." When a recipe calls for egg whites specifically, use the real thing. When a recipe asks you to separate yolks and whites, you may use egg white in place of yolks unless the recipe indicates that you must use whole eggs. (Use the two sets of egg whites separately, as described in the recipe.)

Milk and Other Dairy Products   You may use whole, low-fat, or nonfat milk. The same goes for yogurt, sour cream, ricotta cheese, cottage cheese, and hard cheeses. You may use whole, low-fat, or nonfat cream cheese. Or check out the Mock Cream Cheese on page 90.

Butter or Margarine   These are mostly interchangeable in recipes. If a recipe calls for "butter or margarine," there's usually a reason to use a solid fat rather than a liquid vegetable oil. You may want to use a little less butter or margarine and add an equivalent amount of oil. I don't recommend using reduced-fat butter or margarine in cooking because both are usually made with water, which will alter the composition of your batter or dough. However, by all means use reduced-fat butter or margarine as a spread.

Oil   Any vegetable oil will work in these recipes but it's best to use an unsaturated oil like safflower, soy, or canola. I prefer canola oil because it has almost no taste and so it doesn't interfere with the flavor of the other ingredients.

Flour   Many recipes that specify all-purpose flour can be made with a combination of all-purpose and whole-wheat flours. If your family isn't used to nonwhite flour, they may not be prepared for the heavier texture of foods cooked with whole-wheat or other whole-grain flours, so introduce them slowly. The first time you try a new recipe, you might want to make it using all-purpose flour only. The next time, you might substitute a small portion of whole-wheat flour, adding a little more each time you make the dish.

Because I want my family to get extra fiber in the morning, I usually use half all-purpose flour and half whole-wheat flour or two parts all-purpose flour to one part whole-wheat flour. (More than half whole-wheat flour recipes require additional modification.)

By all means stir some wheat germ into your flour-based recipes if you want. Try adding 2 tablespoons of wheat germ to every cup of flour. If you have a favorite alternative flour, like soy or rye, use these instead of whole-wheat flour in combination with all-purpose flour.

Do pancakes made with egg whites and skim milk, mixed with half whole-wheat flour taste the same as pancakes made with whole eggs, full-fat milk, and all-purpose flour? Hey, is the pope Episcopalian? If you're more accustomed to the traditional versions of recipes like pancakes or blueberry muffins, you may find the low-fat, high-fiber version a bit strange. Educate your palate a little at a time, and you may well come to prefer the more healthful varieties.

Fruit Dishes

Naturally sweet, full of fiber, low in calories . . . fruit is the perfect food for morning. These days, fruit is abundantly available around the world, a far cry from the days when an orange in a child's Christmas stocking was a rare treat.

Nutritionists would prefer that you eat your fruit rather than drink it as juice because the fiber in whole fresh fruit is nutritious and sustaining. However, if you don't like fruit or haven't time for it in the morning, by all means drink juice or try one of the frothy blender drinks in the recipes that follow.

This chapter is divided into three sections: cold fruit, hot fruit, and drinks. More than any other chapter though, this one is really intended to give you ideas for making your own creations. You can't go far wrong with fruits unless you buy ones that aren't ripe and seasonal. So go to the market, buy the best fruit they have, and then look for a recipe that will work with your purchase. Certain fruits can easily be interchanged in most recipes—different types of melon, for instance, apples and pears, varieties of berries, and so on. Tropical fruits tend to go together well as do "winter fruits."

Choose Your Fruit

For tips on choosing fruits I went to my favorite greengrocer, Charlie Paley, of Sharon, Connecticut. The following "who's who" of fruits is based in part on our tour of the fruits he carries in his market.

Apples   A classic autumn fruit (though they're available year-round), apples can be divided into those that taste wonderful when eaten fresh—especially Red and Golden Delicious, Granny Smith, McIntosh, and a new variety, Imperial Gala—and those that make superior cooking apples—Cortlands, Winesaps, Northern Spys, or Rome Beauties. Look for apples with unblemished skin. "Even though apples are harder than other fruits, they can bruise," Charlie points out. "Look for ones that are shiny and clean. Avoid the older-looking ones that feel waxy." Once peeled, apples go brown quickly. So either incorporate them in your salad right away or sprinkle on a little fresh lemon juice, which will prevent the apples from discoloring.

Apricots   They should be firm, not mushy, and have an orangey bloom on their skin. Underripe fruits will be too hard and sour tasting. Your best bet is to buy fruit that has already ripened to perfection on the tree. However, apricots stored at room temperature for a day or two will ripen a little. Apricots perform beautifully in fruit salads; there's no need to remove the skin.

Bananas   Like the song says, "You must never put bananas in the refrigerator, no, no, no, no!" Left out of the refrigerator, hard, yellow-skinned bananas will ripen nicely, so choosing bananas depends on how soon you want to eat them and how ripe you like them. Brown spots on the fruit should not discourage you. Charlie recommends buying bananas when they're green and letting them ripen at home. In his view, they're most delicious when the skins are spotted but not totally brown. Or when they're bright yellow.

Berries   Most berries are quite perishable, so look for perfectly ripe berries and use them right away. Good, rich color is an indication of ripeness, while mushiness is a sure sign of over-ripeness. "Strawberries can be deceptive," Charlie says. "They may look great but not really taste good." With all berries, he recommends judging by smell and, ideally, sneaking out a couple of berries and tasting them. Because berries are very perishable, almost every basket of berries contains a few overripe or underripe berries. When you bring the berries home, rinse them under cool water and pick through them to find the best berries. (This is a good activity for young children.) Dry them gently with a clean cloth towel or paper towel, then trim the stems. You may want to cut strawberries in half or slice them.

Cherries   This sublime fruit is only available in the summer. "Look for good dark color," Charlie says, "and taste one!" Cutting out the pits is a bore; you may be able to find a special tool for this in a kitchen supply shop.

Coconuts   This exotic, intensely flavorful fruit is a great addition to fruit salads. Look for a firm, hairy skin and shake the coconut to make sure it's full of milk. Now get to work. To open, first drive a nail into the bald spots at the base of the coconut and drain out the milk. (Stir a little coconut milk into your fruit salad or use it in blender drinks.) Then turn the coconut on its side on a folded towel and smash it with the hammer. Prizing free the meat from the shell is hard work but worth the effort. Or heat a drained coconut for several minutes in a 350F (175C) oven. Remove from oven and cool. Give it a few taps with the hammer.

Figs   Dried figs used to be more familiar, but these days figs are available in their succulent fresh form. They should be soft to the touch and sweet-smelling; be wary of any sour-smelling figs. Figs are highly sensitive and perishable; buy them in perfect condition and use them as soon as possible.

Grapefruits   The "grapefruit diet" was popular a few years back because the grapefruit has a remarkable ability to curb appetite. "White" (actually pale yellow) grapefruit is less sweet than the attractive pink variety. Avoid grapefruit that feels overly light; it may have dried out. Finally, grapefruit is the opposite of bananas: it should go right into the refrigerator, yes, yes, yes, yes. Look for especially good Florida grapefruits around Christmas.

Grapes   Here again the varieties are almost endless. The important thing is to look for those that are seedless (you don't want to rise at 5:00 A.M. to de-seed your family's grapes!) and that have healthy green stems and plump, firm, and colorful fruit. Grapes don't improve over time, so buy ones that are ready to eat. Look for the elegant tiny champagne grapes, which have the familiar flavor of the bubbly stuff. (When presented with a bunch of grapes, it is good manners to break off a branch and pluck the individual fruit at your own place, not to pull grapes off the communal stem.)

Guavas   You can't tell the worth of a guava by its size or color. Instead look for those that are firm but not hard, heavy, and wonderfully fragrant.

Kiwifruits   To my taste, kiwifruits are more notable for their attractive appearance when sliced and their vitamin C content than for their flavor. Charlie, however, likes them a lot. He recommends looking for kiwifruits that are soft but not too soft—they should have a little give. You can buy them green and let them ripen on your kitchen counter. For fruit salad, peel the fruit and either cut it into wedges or slices.

Mangoes   This sweet, almost buttery fruit is delicious in salads or blender drinks. Look for a tough yellow or orange skin that yields a little when you press on it. Mangoes aren't easy fruits to handle. Charlie recommends making four longitudinal cuts through the skin and meat to the pit, then peeling away the skin and slicing the meat off the pit as closely as you can. Serve slices of mango with wedges of lemon or lime. Charlie likes to crumble a little goat cheese on his.

Melons To test the ripeness of a melon, gently press the circular patch at the base where the melon was cut from the vine. It should be soft but not mushy and should spring back and release a sweet aroma. Melons don't ripen off the vine. They're either ready to eat or not ripe enough. The most popular are the very sweet watermelon (look for the new seedless varieties), the cantaloupe (orange fruit, peachy skin), and the honeydew (pale green fruit and skin). By all means experiment with other varieties. Once you've cut a melon open, the flavor tends to dominate everything around it, so double wrap before putting an opened melon in the refrigerator.

Nectarines A close cousin to the peach; use the same criteria as for peaches for choosing ripe ones.

Oranges There seems to be an endless variety of oranges available these days. To simplify your cooking, shop for a seedless variety with a slightly loose skin that will be easy to peel. As with any citrus fruit, judge an orange by its weight: if it's too light, it has probably dried out. You can't tell much from the color of an orange because they're usually dyed. Wait until the produce clerk is looking the other way and then squeeze and sniff—a ripe orange will be firm but fragrant. Small varieties, like satsumas, clementines, and tangerines, tend to be sweeter and look lovely in fruit salad. When you've peeled an orange (or other citrus fruit), strip away excess pith (the white stringy bits clinging to the fruit). If a recipe calls for "zest," rinse and dry the skin of the fruit, then use a vegetable grater or a zester to scrape off only the colorful part of the skin.

Papayas The skin of a ripe papaya will have turned from green to yellow; the fruit will be orange. The black seeds of the papaya are edible. If you like their rather peppery taste, you may want to toss some over the top of a fruit salad as a garnish.

Peaches These summer favorites won't ripen on your windowsill, so only buy those that are ripe at the market. (They will soften a little, though.) Look for firm but not hard varieties with good color and fragrance, and inspect them carefully for signs of bruising. To peel a peach, blanch it first for a minute in boiling water, then run under cold water while stripping away the peel.

Pears   The varieties of pears are theoretically seasonal, although these days you can usually get a decent pear at any time of year. Look for slightly soft (but not bruised) and fragrant fruits. Leave them out to ripen at room temperature.

Pineapples   To test for ripeness, pull on the leaves at the top of the pineapple. They should be loose but not so loose that they come off in your hand. Also, the circular scar at the base of the pineapple should be soft and should release a pleasing smell when pressed, but it should not be moldy or smell fermented. The newest variety, gold pineapples, are sweeter and more reliable than their conventional cousins.

Plums   You can't tell a good plum by its smell at the market, so look for varieties that are soft but not too soft and have good color. Plums will ripen quickly on your counter or more slowly in the refrigerator.

Pomegranates   The seeds of this most sensuous of fruits make a beautiful and crunchy addition to fruit dishes. Look for deep-red, almost maroon-skinned fruits. Cut the pomegranate into quarters and then separate into sections and gently pry out the seeds. Some cooks like to do this in a bowl of water to avoid being sprayed by the juice.

Make It Beautiful

In addition to tasting delicious, fruit should look lovely, too. As you make your own combinations, look for ways to present contrasting colors, shapes, and textures. How you cut fruit makes a big difference to its overall appearance. Here are some ideas that are popular for special breakfasts and brunches:

Apple Roses   Carefully peel a long, thin strip of apple peel. Brush the inside of the peel with lemon juice to prevent browning. Now tightly wind the peel around itself into a flower and stick a wooden pick right through the peel to hold it in place.

Cherry Flowers   You can make a pretty garnish for fruit salads by slicing down the sides of a cherry, removing the pit and fanning out the resulting "petals" into a flower shape.

Citrus Flowers   Score deep lengthwise grooves along the circumference of a lemon, lime, or orange. Now slice the fruit crosswise for pretty round "flowers."

Citrus Twists   Leaving the skin on, cut thin slices of orange, lemon, or lime. Make a cut from the center of each slice through the peel. Twist the slice and stand on its own— either on top of a fruit salad or around the circumference of a bowl, or use as a garnish with eggs or other dishes.

Edible Flowers   With their vivid colors, edible flowers make lovely garnishes. You may scatter individual petals onto your fruit salad or toss on a few blossoms. Look for calendula, chives, day lilies, lavender, nasturtium, sunflowers, violas (Johnny-jump-ups), and zucchini. Some edible flowers are more flavorful than others. For more information on edible flowers, I recommend a charming book: *Edible Flowers: A Kitchen Companion* by Kitty Morse (Ten Speed Press, 1995).

Fruit Wheels   Many people who don't especially care for fruit salad prefer thinly sliced fruit served in elegant simplicity in its own natural juice. On a beautiful plate, arrange thin slices of melon, apple, and pineapple in a wheel. You might put a cherry or strawberry flower in the middle.

Melon or Pineapple Baskets   Stand the pineapple or melon upright or, if using a watermelon, on its side. (The pineapple can be placed on its side too.) Cut down on either side of a central "handle" and then across the sides of the "basket." Now hollow out the underside of the "handle" and the interior so that the "basket" can be filled with fruit salad. Similar ideas include "boats" and "bowls." (Instead of cutting on a line, you might choose a scalloped or jagged edge.)

Melon Balls   Apart from a good sharp knife, a melon baller (available in most kitchen shops) is your most essential piece of fruit-salad equipment. Find one with a different size "baller" on either end. Fill a champagne glass or parfait dish with assorted melon balls and garnish with sprigs of mint.

Orange Cups   Instead of peeling an orange, take a sharp knife and cut around the orange, either in a single straight line or in an interesting pattern. Gently pull the fruit apart, remove the sections and scrape out any excess pith. Serve fruit salad in each cup. Or, cut away the top third of the orange, fill the hollowed shell and then replace the "hat" on top. (The latter approach is especially popular with young children.)

Pineapple Rings and Chains   To make pineapple rings, cut away the skin of a pineapple, slice crosswise, and use a sharp round cookie cutter to remove the tough core of each slice. Cut each ring once from the hole at the center to one edge and slip pieces through each other to form a chain. Use the chain to encircle a serving dish and mound fruit salad in the middle.

Strawberry Flowers   Slice off the cap of a strawberry and stand it on end. Now cut wedges through the tip and gently bend down to form a flower.

About Fruit Salads

When making your own fruit salad, look for colors that harmonize well together. You may want to go for a subtle palette of pastels (see the Gingered Melon on page 21) or for a riot of colors (like the Ambrosia on page 22). Think about texture, too. You may choose fruits with similar textures, but you're more likely to enjoy a variety. Firm fruits like apples and pears will balance softer ones like kiwifruits and nectarines and keep the salad from getting mushy.

When making a dressing for a fruit salad, use subtle flavors that don't overwhelm the fruits' natural fragrance and sweetness. Don't overdress a fruit salad—you don't want it to become soggy. Finally, make sure the flavors of the fruits work well together. Contrasts of sweet fruit like banana with more acidic fruit like pineapple are always successful, but you may want to try subtler combinations, like the Honeyed Fruit Salad on page 23.

About Hot Fruit Dishes

On cold winter mornings, a hot fruit dish may well be more appealing than a cold fruit salad. When fruit is cooked—even if it's only grilled briefly—it softens and the fiber breaks down a little so that the fruit is a bit more readily digested. A fruit that is a little too soft to eat cold may be fine in a hot fruit dish. Hot fruit is especially delicious with cold yogurt, cottage cheese, or milk.

About Fruit Drinks

My sister Caitlin Flanagan lives in Los Angeles, the undisputed world capital of blender drinks. I bow to her superior knowledge in offering you her time-honored tips:

- One's happiness with one's blender drinks is going to be directly proportional not to the ingredients (you can't go wrong, as long as you don't add gravy or baked beans) but to the quality of one's blender. If the blender balks at a few ice cubes and grinds and groans, and never really gets them fully pulverized, the whole thing will be onerous. On the other hand, if it is a high-quality blender designed to accommodate ice cubes, making blender drinks will be a pleasure.

- The advent of those multijuice combos that are available in cartons makes smoothies ridiculously easy. You will see these items next to the regular orange juice cartons in the dairy section of any fine grocery store.
- Let me state that although blender drinks are usually very healthy and can be very low in fat, they tend *not* to be low-calorie. People often think they are good for dieting because they do tend to have healthful ingredients, but fruit juices are relatively caloric, as are the other ingredients that often go into these drinks. As a main course for breakfast, a blender drink is fine, but I wouldn't serve one with pancakes and eggs.

What more can I add, except to emphasize that making blender drinks calls for creativity. If there are fresh plums at your market, throw them in the blender. Do you love peanut butter? Throw a spoonful of that in, too. Use the recipes that follow to get the hang of it and then go wild!

Honey-Yogurt Fruit Salad

This creamy base goes well with virtually any fruit. This combination is just a suggestion.

MAKES ABOUT 2 1/2 CUPS.

1/2 cup low-fat yogurt

1 to 2 teaspoons honey

2 cups of fruit: diced pineapple, sliced
   banana, diced apple, sliced nectarine,
   halved strawberries, sliced kiwifruit,
   blueberries or raspberries

1/4 cup chopped nuts

In a large bowl, mix yogurt and honey and blend well. Stir in fruits and sprinkle nuts on top.

Variations

Instead of plain yogurt and honey, use your favorite flavored yogurt: lemon, strawberry, and vanilla are all good choices. Finally, if the fruit you choose is naturally sweet enough, you can easily reduce or eliminate the honey.

Gingered Melon

The tangy taste of fresh ginger is an excellent foil for sweet, juicy melon. Alternatively, the ginger sauce works nicely with tropical combinations like pineapple, papaya, and banana.

MAKES ABOUT 2 CUPS.

4 (1/4-inch-thick) slices peeled ginger root
2 whole cloves
1 cinnamon stick
1 tablespoon sugar

1/2 cup water
2 cups chopped or balled assorted melons:
    cantaloupe, honeydew, and watermelon

In a saucepan, combine the ginger slices, cloves, cinnamon stick, sugar, and water. Simmer over medium-low heat about 15 minutes. Strain the mixture into a bowl and let it cool to room temperature. Reserve 2 slices of ginger and cut them into thin strips; discard remaining spices.

In a large bowl, lightly toss the cooled ginger sauce with the melon. Sprinkle with the reserved ginger slices and refrigerate at least 1 hour before serving.

Variation

Garnish with sliced fresh or canned litchi nuts.

Ambrosia

This recipe for the "food of the Gods" doesn't contain miniature marshmallows, but if that's your idea of heaven, by all means, sprinkle some on! I like to think that the Olympians found the succulent tropical fruits—and their own company—simply divine.

MAKES ABOUT 3 CUPS.

2 cups fresh fruit: diced papaya, sectioned seedless satsuma oranges, sliced ripe banana, green and/or red grapes, diced pineapple, diced red or golden Delicious apple
2 tablespoons orange juice
1/2 cup plain yogurt

1/4 cup sweetened or unsweetened grated coconut
1 to 2 tablespoons honey
Pinch of ground ginger
Pinch of ground nutmeg
2 tablespoons almond slices (optional), toasted (see Note below)

In a large bowl, gently toss together the fruit and orange juice.

In a small bowl, mix yogurt, coconut, honey, ginger, and nutmeg. Add this mixture to the fruit and gently toss. Sprinkle with almond slices, if using. Serve at once or refrigerate up to 2 hours.

Note

To toast almonds or other nuts, spread nuts in a baking pan and toast in a preheated 350F (175C) oven about 5 minutes or until golden.

Honeyed Fruit Salad

The sweet taste of honey and the pungent flavor of herbal tea work beautifully in combination with slightly tart fruits. This fruit salad is lightly dressed; for more syrup, double the amounts of tea and honey.

MAKES ABOUT 3 CUPS.

2 tablespoons boiling water
1 fruit-flavored tea bag
2 tablespoons honey
1 cup hulled, sliced strawberries

1 cup other berries in season (blueberries, raspberries, blackberries, etc.)
2 nectarines, sliced
1 Granny Smith apple, diced

In a mug, pour boiling water over tea bag. Let steep 3 minutes. Remove the tea bag and stir in the honey. Let the mixture cool.

Put the fruits in a bowl and add the honey-tea mixture. Toss gently, being careful not to bruise the berries and nectarines. Pour the fruit salad into a beautiful bowl and serve or refrigerate up to 2 hours.

Variation

If you like chamomile tea, use it instead of fruit-flavored tea.

Minted Fruit Salad

This delicately flavored fruit salad is served at the Captain Dibbell House in Clinton, Connecticut.

MAKES ABOUT 4 CUPS.

2 tablespoons sugar
2 tablespoons orange juice
2 tablespoons fresh lemon juice
2 tablespoons water
2 drops peppermint extract
4 cups assorted chopped fresh fruit:
   ripe melons, kiwifruit, apples, grapefruit,
   oranges, bananas, etc.

Fresh mint leaves
Edible flowers: Johnny-jump-ups,
   nasturtiums, calendulas

In a small bowl, combine the sugar, juices, water, and peppermint extract. Stir until the sugar dissolves.

Place the fruit in a large, shallow serving dish and pour the juice mixture over the fruit. Cover and chill 3 hours or overnight, stirring occasionally.

To serve, scatter fresh mint leaves over the top and garnish with flowers.

Peaches and "Cream"

In season, there is nothing like fresh peaches. Here's a way to revamp an old favorite.

MAKES 4 SERVINGS.

1/2 cup ricotta cheese, drained
2 tablespoons milk
1/4 teaspoon pure vanilla extract
1 tablespoon sugar (optional)
1 tablespoon hulled sunflower kernels
   (optional)

4 ripe peaches, peeled and sliced
   lengthwise
4 citrus twists (see page 16)

Put ricotta cheese, milk, vanilla, and sugar, if using, in a blender and blend for about 2 minutes or until frothy. Pour the "cream" into a bowl and stir in the sunflower kernels, if using. Gently toss in the peaches.

Spoon into 4 parfait glasses and place a citrus twist on top of each. Eat at once or refrigerate up to 2 hours.

Avocado-Citrus Salad

You might not think of avocado at the breakfast table. It is, however, technically a fruit and it teams beautifully with citrus.

MAKES 4 SERVINGS.

1 tablespoon olive oil
1 teaspoon fresh lemon juice
1 teaspoon finely chopped fresh tarragon
Salt and pepper to taste

1 navel orange, sectioned
1 grapefruit, sectioned
1 firm, ripe avocado, cut lengthwise into
   thin slices

In a small bowl, whisk together olive oil, lemon juice, tarragon, salt, and pepper.

On 4 plates, create a pattern of alternating orange, grapefruit, and avocado slices, radiating from the center of the plate. Spoon on the dressing and serve at once.

Variation

Melon also pairs nicely with avocado. You can use your melon baller on avocado for a melon-avocado salad, or try a cantaloupe, honeydew, and avocado plate.

Figgy Pudding

This probably isn't precisely what the Christmas carolers have in mind when they sing "we all want some figgy pudding." It is, however, a light, fragrant fruit compote that uses winter fruits to advantage.

MAKES 4 TO 6 SERVINGS.

1 teaspoon grated lemon zest
1 teaspoon grated orange zest
1/4 cup apple juice
1/4 cup white grape juice
1/4 cup sugar
1/2 teaspoon ground cinnamon
4 cardamom pods

4 whole cloves
1 Golden Delicious apple, cut into wedges
1 Granny Smith apple, cut into wedges
2 ripe pears (different varieties), cut into wedges
2 satsuma oranges, sectioned
4 fresh figs, cut into wedges

Combine the citrus zest, juices, sugar, and spices in a medium saucepan. Simmer, stirring until sugar dissolves, over low heat about 5 minutes to make a thin syrup.

Put all the fruits except the figs into a 2-quart casserole dish. Pour the syrup over the fruit, toss lightly, and bake 30 minutes, until the fruit is softened but not mushy.

Remove from the oven. Discard the cardamom pods and cloves. Place the figs on top of the other fruits, cover the casserole dish, and let stand 15 minutes so that the figs can be heated without overcooking. Serve warm.

Variation

If you cannot find fresh figs, use dried figs and add them to the casserole 15 minutes before removing from the oven.

Baked Bananas

Naturally sweet, nutritious, and delicious, bananas make an excellent main course. Serve this simple dish with yogurt and sprinkle on some homemade granola (page 59).

MAKES 2 SERVINGS.

2 teaspoons butter   2 teaspoons brown sugar
2 bananas

Preheat oven to 350F (175C). Spray an 8- or 9-inch-round or -square nonstick baking dish with cooking spray. Put the butter in the dish and warm in the oven 5 minutes or until it is hot and melted.

   Peel and slice each banana into quarters by cutting each in half lengthwise and then crosswise. Gently roll the banana slices in the melted butter, then arrange them in the pan with the rounded sides up. Sprinkle with the brown sugar and bake about 20 minutes or until bananas are hot and sugar is melted. Serve at once.

Variation

For a fat-free version, omit the butter. Leave the skin on the bananas, quarter as described above and bake with the skin side down. You may also eliminate the sugar, for a no-sugar-added variation. Peel banana before serving.

"Little Fruit Things"

This recipe comes from Peg Dumbro of the Hillcrest Guest House in Rutland, Vermont. She thought she'd made up the idea for "little fruit things" herself until she discovered that she'd "invented" a breakfast version of Italian bruschetta. Anyhow, I like her version.

MAKES 4 SERVINGS.

4 slices sturdy country-style bread
1 teaspoon butter or margarine
2 pears, apples, plums, or a combination
   of fruit, sliced
4 teaspoons apricot jam

4 heaping tablespoons blueberries or
   raspberries
1/4 teaspoon ground cinnamon
1 teaspoon sugar (optional)

Preheat the broiler. Spread slices of bread lightly with butter or margarine. Arrange the fruit slices in a wheel on the slices of bread. (Alternating fruits works nicely.) Place a dollop of jam in the center of each fruit wheel. Dot berries around fruit and jam. Sprinkle with cinnamon and sugar, if using.

    Broil 5 to 10 minutes or until the bread looks toasted and the fruit is hot and wilted.

Variations

You may want to dot additional butter or margarine on the fruit before broiling. Try other varieties of fruit, such as peaches, bananas, or strawberries. Instead of slicing the fruit, finely dice it and spread it on the toast.

Baked Apples

You don't have to get fancy with baked apples; they're delicious plain (baked with just a little brown sugar and cinnamon, for instance) or dressed up, as they are below. Baked apples reheat nicely: you can make them the night before and zap them back to life in the microwave in the morning, if you like. They're delightful cold, too. Hot or cold, a dollop of yogurt is a good accompaniment.

MAKES 4 BAKED APPLES.

4 large cooking apples

1/3 cup chopped walnuts

1/3 cup raisins or currants

1/4 cup packed brown sugar (optional)

1 tablespoon fresh lemon juice

1 teaspoon ground allspice

Preheat the oven to 350F (175C). Core the apples, being careful not to cut right through the bottoms. Peel away about an inch of skin around the top of each apple.

Combine the remaining ingredients and stuff them into the wells left by the apple cores. Set the apples in a small baking dish and pour in enough boiling water to come about halfway up the apples.

Bake 45 to 55 minutes or until tender but not mushy. Baste occasionally with the water and juices in the pan.

Variations

If you're feeling reckless, you might dot the tops of the nut-fruit mixture with butter. Or instead of the walnut-fruit mixture, heap in your favorite granola. Another time, mix 2 tablespoons dried cranberries or dried cherries into the walnut-sugar mixture.

At the Black Friar Inn, in Bar Harbor, Maine, they serve baked apples poached in apple cider or cranberry juice instead of water—delicious!

Hot Spiced Plums

This dish is fabulous on its own, served with Fake Cream (page 91), or as a topping for pancakes, waffles, or French toast.

MAKES ABOUT 2 CUPS.

1 pound ripe plums, cut into small wedges
1/4 teaspoon ground cinnamon

1/8 teaspoon ground ginger
2 tablespoons sugar (optional)

Place the plums in a large nonstick frying pan and sprinkle with the cinnamon, ginger, and sugar, if using. Sauté over medium-low heat, stirring occasionally, until the plums are softened but not mushy. Serve at once.

Baked Grapefruit

For a simple grilled grapefruit, just sprinkle brown sugar and a few dots of butter or margarine on a grapefruit half and broil for 5 to 10 minutes or until the sugar is melted and bubbly. Here's a more elaborate treatment which is attractive and easy to eat.

MAKES 4 SERVINGS.

1 pink grapefruit	4 teaspoons brown sugar (optional)
1 white grapefruit	2 teaspoons butter (optional)
1 orange	4 teaspoons pomegranate seeds

Preheat oven to 400F (205C). Cut the grapefruits in half crosswise. Carefully remove sections without poking holes in the skins. Remove pith and break fruit into sections. Peel the orange and remove pith. Cut orange in half crosswise and break fruit into sections.

In a medium bowl, gently toss grapefruit and orange sections and mound into the grapefruit skins. Sprinkle with brown sugar and dot with butter, if using.

Bake 15 to 20 minutes or until the fruit is hot, bubbly, and lightly browned. Sprinkle with pomegranate seeds and serve.

Variation

For spicy baked grapefruit, sprinkle on a little nutmeg and/or ginger.

Fruit Kabobs

If you're feeling ambitious one weekend, you might try making these kabobs on the barbecue. Weekdays, cooking them quickly under the broiler will be just as good. The glaze is optional; fruit kabobs are mighty good on their own. Basting with the glaze keeps the fruit from drying out and brings out their flavors beautifully.

MAKES 8 KABOBS.

1 to 2 firm bananas, cut crosswise into
    thick slices
1/4 cantaloupe, cut into chunks
1/2 small pineapple, cut into chunks
1 orange or grapefruit, sectioned

Glaze (optional)
1/4 cup packed brown sugar
1 teaspoon butter or margarine
2 tablespoons water

Preheat the broiler to its highest temperature.

Skewer the fruits on 8 metal skewers, alternating fruits.

To make the optional glaze, melt butter or margarine in a small saucepan over low heat, then add brown sugar and water and cook, stirring, until the brown sugar is completely dissolved.

Using a pastry brush, baste the fruit with the glaze. Broil 5 to 10 minutes, basting once again halfway through cooking. Keep an eye on the kabobs; they're ready when the fruit has softened and browned but not blackened. Serve at once.

Variation

Instead of the glaze, baste the fruit with maple syrup.

Aunt Katie's Fruit Drink

From the blender-drink maven herself, here's a smoothie with L.A. style.

MAKES 2 DRINKS, ABOUT 8 OUNCES EACH.

1 cup chilled fruit salad in natural juices
1/2 cup frozen vanilla yogurt
1/2 cup fruit juice combination (such as
 guava-mango nectar)

1 teaspoon pure vanilla extract

Put all the ingredients into the blender and process until smooth.

Buttermilk-Fruit Drink

This drink is rich and frothy but very low fat.

MAKES 2 DRINKS, ABOUT 8 OUNCES EACH.

1 1/4 cups mixed fruit juices (such as
 orange-banana-pineapple)
3/4 cup buttermilk

2 ice cubes
1 tablespoon strawberry preserves

Put all the ingredients into the blender and process until the ice has been crushed.

Exotic Papaya Surprise

It's the spices that make this drink exotic; experiment to see how surprising you want it to be!

MAKES 2 DRINKS, ABOUT 8 OUNCES EACH.

2 ripe papayas, cut into chunks
1/2 cup orange juice
1/2 cup milk
1 teaspoon honey (optional)

Pinch of ground ginger
Pinch of ground cinnamon
2 to 4 ice cubes

Put all the ingredients into the blender and process until the ice has been crushed.

Variation

For an even thicker version, use buttermilk or yogurt in place of milk.

Icy Banana Drink

Here's something special for a morning boost.

MAKES 2 DRINKS, ABOUT 8 OUNCES EACH.

1/4 cup frozen orange juice concentrate
1/2 peeled ripe banana
3/4 cup vanilla frozen yogurt

1/4 cup nonfat dry milk
4 ice cubes

Put all the ingredients into the blender and process until the ice has been crushed.

Peach-Berry Smoothie

This tasty drink whips up into a beautiful purple color.

MAKES 2 DRINKS, ABOUT 8 OUNCES EACH.

2 peaches, cut into wedges
1/3 cup mixed blackberries and halved
   strawberries
1/3 cup plain yogurt
1/2 cup milk

1 tablespoon sugar (optional)
1 tablespoon wheat germ (optional)
1/2 teaspoon pure vanilla extract
3 ice cubes

Put all the ingredients into the blender and process until the ice is crushed.

Orange Sunrise

For a beautiful presentation, take this tip from the Black Friar Inn in Bar Harbor, Maine. The exact proportions depend on the size of the glass. The result looks like a tequila sunrise.

MAKES 1 (8-OUNCE) DRINK.

3/4 glass chilled orange juice with pulp

1/4 glass chilled cranberry juice cocktail

Fill an elegant glass about three quarters full of orange juice. Carefully fill the rest of the way with chilled cranberry juice.

Variation

Float a sprig of mint on top.

Sorbet Smoothies

To me, sorbet-based smoothies are the ultimate in blender drinks. They take a little extra planning, but if you get in the habit of making sorbet (an extremely rewarding pursuit), you'll always have some in the freezer.

MAKES 2 DRINKS, A LITTLE OVER 8 OUNCES EACH.

1 cup Mango Sorbet (page 95)   1/2 cup milk
1/2 cup plain yogurt   1/2 ripe banana

Combine all ingredients in the blender and process until smooth and icy.

Variations

Strawberry Smoothie

Substitute Strawberry Sorbet (page 96) for the Mango Sorbet, strawberry yogurt for the plain yogurt, and a peeled and sliced peach for the banana.

Try a combination of mango and strawberry sorbet and/or other sorbets.

Frothy Watermelon Drink

A change from dairy-based smoothies, this completely natural drink is sparklingly refreshing.

MAKES 2 DRINKS, ABOUT 8 OUNCES EACH.

2 cups seedless watermelon chunks
1/4 cup apple or pineapple juice
  concentrate

4 ice cubes
1/4 cup sparkling water

Put the watermelon, juice concentrate, and ice cubes into the blender and process until the ice is crushed. Dilute the mixture with sparkling water to taste.

The Creative Bakery

There's nothing like biting into a warm muffin or slice of quick bread first thing in the morning. It makes getting out of bed worth the effort. Furthermore, if there are any breakfast-skippers in your household, the smell of fresh baking is sure to overcome their resistance.

The recipes that follow are varied, from Southern spoon bread to carrot-cranberry muffins to Irish soda bread. Most are low in fat and sugar but none is fat free. To my mind, a little fat provides the flavor you crave within the guidelines of healthy eating. Serve the bread or muffin without butter or margarine and you won't upset your diet . . . unless you can't resist eating the whole batch!

Breads and muffins taste best when they're fresh from the oven, but it's hard to find the time in the morning to prepare them. Here are some ways to get around that problem:

Prepare All Your Ingredients the Night Before!

Most bread and muffin batters can't be made completely the night before because the leavening agents lose their strength. You can, however, mix up all the dry ingredients and leave them, covered, on the kitchen counter overnight. Mix up the liquid ingredients in another bowl, cover and refrigerate them. You might even prepare the muffin cups or loaf pans. (If you're using grease, you should refrigerate the cups or pans, then take them out when you preheat the oven in the morning.)

In the morning, making fresh bread or muffins is a simple matter of adding the liquid ingredients to the dry ones, pouring the batter into the prepared pans and sliding the pans into the oven!

Seal It!

Alternatively, you can make your life simpler by making your breads or muffins at a calmer time of day. Most breads and muffins will keep nicely out of the freezer for at least 24 hours. Before sealing them, make sure they have cooled completely to room temperature. Then store in an airtight container or double wrap in plastic wrap and foil. Keeping them in the refrigerator will help keep them fresh, though they'll be uninvitingly cold in the morning. If you have time, warm them up a little before serving.

Freeze It!

If you want to save bread or muffins for more than twenty-four hours, your best bet is to freeze them. Again, make sure the bread or muffins have cooled down completely to room temperature before you freeze them. Next, wrap well, first in a plastic wrap and then a double layer of foil. You may want to wrap muffins individually or slice bread and wrap individual slices. Use freezer tape to date and identify the contents. The night before you plan to use them, take the baked goods out of the freezer and leave them on the counter overnight. If you have time, warm them up a little before serving. Use frozen breads or muffins within six weeks of baking.

Baking Hints

Before you begin baking, please review the note "A Word About Ingredients" on pages 8 and 9. It will help you decide whether to use whole eggs or egg substitute, skim or whole milk, etc. One final note: to prepare muffin cups, either line cups with paper liners or spray nonstick pans with nonstick cooking spray.

High Meadows Apple-Strudel Muffins

Here's a wholesome variation on apple strudel, from the High Meadows Vineyard and Mountain Sunset in Albemarle County, Virginia.

MAKES 12 MUFFINS.

Strudel Topping (see opposite)
2 1/4 cups all-purpose flour
1/4 to 1/2 cup sugar
2 teaspoons baking powder
1 teaspoon baking soda
1/4 teaspoon salt
1 teaspoon ground cinnamon
2 eggs
1/2 cup vegetable oil
1 1/2 cups dried apple with skins on,
   finely chopped

1/2 cup currants
1/2 cup plain yogurt

Strudel Topping
1/2 cup chopped walnuts
3 tablespoons all-purpose flour
3 tablespoons butter or margarine
3 tablespoons sugar
1 teaspoon ground cinnamon

Preheat oven to 400F (205C). Spray 12 muffin cups with nonstick cooking spray.

Prepare topping: In a small bowl, mix together the topping ingredients until all the walnut pieces are coated. Set aside.

In a large bowl, mix together the flour, sugar, baking powder, baking soda, salt, and cinnamon.

In another bowl, beat the eggs until light. Stir in the oil, then the dried apples and currants and finally the yogurt. Gently fold the liquid ingredients into the dry ones just until mixed.

Spoon the mixture into the prepared muffin cups and top each muffin with 1 to 2 teaspoons of the topping mixture. Bake 25 minutes until golden. Turn out muffins onto a wire rack. Serve warm or at room temperature.

Corn-Flake Muffins

These tasty muffins have the flavor of traditional corn muffins but are lighter and less grainy.

MAKES 12 MUFFINS.

1 1/2 cups all-purpose flour
1/3 cup sugar (optional)
2 1/2 teaspoons baking powder
1/2 teaspoon baking soda
1/4 teaspoon salt

2 1/4 cups corn flakes
1 1/3 cups milk
1 egg
3 tablespoons vegetable oil

Preheat oven to 400F (205C). Spray 12 muffin cups with nonstick cooking spray.

In a medium bowl, mix together the flour, sugar, if using, baking powder, baking soda, and salt.

Pour the corn flakes into a large bowl. Use a potato masher to lightly crush the flakes.

In a small bowl, beat together the milk, egg, and oil and pour this mixture over the corn flakes. Stir and let stand about 5 minutes. Fold in the flour mixture just until mixed.

Spoon the batter into prepared muffin cups. Bake about 25 minutes or until golden. Turn out muffins onto a wire rack. Serve warm or at room temperature.

Windermere Carrot and Cranberry Mini Muffins

These succulent morsels are served at Windermere Manor, an elegant bed and breakfast on Lake Arrowhead, in California.

MAKES 24 MINI MUFFINS OR 12 MINI BUNDTS.

1 1/4 cups all-purpose flour
1 teaspoon baking powder
1/2 teaspoon salt
1 teaspoon ground cinnamon
2 eggs
3/4 cup honey

1/4 cup water
1/4 cup vegetable oil
1 1/2 cups shredded carrots
1/4 cup dried cranberries
1/4 cup chopped pecans

Preheat oven to 400F (205C). Spray 24 mini-muffin cups or 12 mini-Bundt pans.

In a large bowl, mix together the flour, baking powder, salt, and cinnamon.

In a medium bowl, beat the eggs until light and stir in the honey, water, and oil. Add liquid ingredients to the dry ingredients and mix just until combined. Fold in the carrots, cranberries, and pecans.

Spoon the batter into prepared muffin cups. Bake 20 minutes or until a wooden pick comes out clean. Turn out muffins onto a wire rack. Serve warm or at room temperature.

Variation

Innkeeper Judee Evers frosts these muffins with an undeniably delicious glaze made by mixing 1/2 cup powdered sugar, 1/4 cup half and half, and 1 teaspoon vanilla extract. The glaze is not necessary—the muffins are sweet and tasty on their own—but you may want to try it one indulgent morning!

Round Barn Farm Rhubarb Muffins

At The Inn at Round Barn Farm, in Waitsfield, Vermont, innkeeper Anne Marie DeFreest gathers rhubarb in early June and freezes it to use year-round.

MAKES 12 SMALL MUFFINS.

Topping (see opposite)
1 egg
1/2 to 3/4 cup packed brown sugar
1/4 cup vegetable oil
1 teaspoon pure vanilla extract
1/2 cup buttermilk
3/4 cup diced rhubarb
1 1/4 cups all-purpose flour
1/2 teaspoon baking soda

1/2 teaspoon baking powder
1/2 teaspoon salt

Topping (optional)
1 1/2 teaspoons butter, melted
1/4 cup sugar
1 teaspoon ground cinnamon
1/4 cup chopped nuts

Preheat the oven to 400F (205C). Spray 12 muffin cups with nonstick cooking spray.

Make the topping, if using: In a small bowl, combine the topping ingredients until the nuts are coated. Set aside.

In a large bowl, beat the egg until light and beat in the brown sugar, oil, vanilla, and buttermilk. Stir in the rhubarb.

In a medium bowl, stir together the flour, baking soda, baking powder, and salt. Add the dry ingredients to the liquid ingredients and stir until well blended. Spoon into prepared muffin cups and sprinkle each muffin with topping mixture.

Bake 20 minutes or until a wooden pick comes out clean. Turn out muffins onto a wire rack. Serve warm or at room temperature.

Variation

If you run out of rhubarb in the middle of winter, substitute frozen raspberries.

Old-Fashioned Blueberry Muffins

This revamped 1950s-style recipe yields a biscuity batter that is a refreshing change from the usual cake muffin.

MAKES 12 MUFFINS.

2 1/4 cups all-purpose flour
2 1/4 teaspoons baking powder
1/2 teaspoon salt
1/4 cup sugar

2 eggs, separated
1 cup milk
1/4 cup vegetable oil
1 cup blueberries

Preheat the oven to 350F (175C). Spray 12 muffin cups with nonstick cooking spray.

In a large bowl, mix together the flour, baking powder, salt, and sugar.

In a smaller bowl, beat the egg yolks, milk, and oil. Stir in the blueberries. Add liquid ingredients to dry ingredients and stir until blended. Beat the egg whites until stiff but not dry. Fold the egg whites into the batter.

Spoon the batter into prepared muffin pans. Bake 20 to 25 minutes or until a wooden pick comes out clean. Turn out muffins onto a wire rack. Serve muffins warm or at room temperature.

Variation

Mash half the blueberries for a different texture.

Maples Inn Gingerbread Muffins

This recipe comes from the Maples Inn in Bar Harbor, Maine. Molasses gives the gingerbread muffins their distinctive dark color and rich flavor.

MAKES 12 MUFFINS.

2 cups all-purpose flour
1/4 to 1/2 cup sugar
1 teaspoon baking soda
1/4 teaspoon salt
1 teaspoon ground cinnamon
1 teaspoon ground ginger

1/4 teaspoon ground nutmeg
3/4 cup chopped nuts (optional)
1 egg
2/3 cup molasses
3/4 cup buttermilk
1/4 cup vegetable oil

Preheat oven to 350F (175C). Spray 12 muffin cups with nonstick cooking spray.

In a medium bowl, combine the flour, sugar, baking soda, salt, and spices, and stir in the nuts, if using.

In a large bowl, beat the egg until light and stir in the molasses, buttermilk, and oil. Stir the dry ingredients into the liquid ingredients and mix just until blended.

Spoon the batter into prepared muffin pans. Bake 20 to 25 minutes or until a wooden pick comes out clean. Turn out muffins onto a wire rack. Serve muffins warm or at room temperature.

Buttermilk Cornmeal Muffins

Here's a low-fat retelling of this classic muffin.

MAKES 12 MUFFINS.

1 cup all-purpose flour
1 cup cornmeal
1/4 cup sugar (optional)
2 1/2 teaspoons baking powder
1/4 teaspoon baking soda

1/2 teaspoon salt
1 egg, beaten
1/4 cup vegetable oil
3/4 cup buttermilk

Preheat oven to 400F (205C). Spray 12 muffin cups with nonstick cooking spray.

In a large bowl, mix the flour, cornmeal, sugar, if using, baking powder, baking soda, and salt.

In a large measuring cup, mix the egg, oil, and buttermilk.

Add the liquid ingredients to the dry ingredients and stir just until blended.

Spoon the batter into prepared muffin pans. Bake about 20 minutes or until lightly browned and a wooden pick comes out clean. Turn out muffins onto a wire rack. Serve warm or at room temperature.

Variations

For double-corn muffins, stir 1/2 cup cooked, drained corn kernels into the batter. For spicier muffins, stir in 1 to 2 tablespoons diced mild or hot chiles. Try sprinkling the tops of the muffins with grated hard cheese (such as Cheddar) or crisscross strips of ham across each muffin before baking.

Oatmeal Scones

These hearty scones are more substantial than classic English tea scones. The texture and flavor will remind you of oatmeal cookies.

MAKES 6 SCONES.

1 1/4 cups all-purpose flour
1 1/4 cups quick-cooking rolled oats
1 teaspoon baking powder
1/2 teaspoon salt
1/4 teaspoon ground cinnamon

1/3 cup packed brown sugar
1/4 cup butter or margarine
1 egg
2/3 cup buttermilk
2/3 cup currants

Preheat the oven to 400F (205C). Spray an 8-inch-round cake pan with nonstick cooking spray.

In a large bowl, mix together the flour, oats, baking powder, salt, cinnamon, and sugar. Work the butter or margarine into the dough with your fingertips until crumbly.

In a small bowl, beat the egg until light and mix in the buttermilk. Add liquid ingredients to the dry ingredients and stir until barely blended. Fold in the currants.

Press the dough into prepared pan and score the top with a sharp knife into 6 wedges.

Bake 30 minutes or until lightly browned. Turn out onto a wire rack and cool. Turn back onto a plate and cut through scoring to form 6 scones.

Popovers

Popovers are easy (providing you follow the directions exactly) and elegant—a real showpiece at the breakfast table. In the oven, these simple rolls burst up and out of the muffin cups to form their characteristic shape.

MAKES 12 POPOVERS.

1 cup all-purpose flour	2 eggs (no substitution)
1/2 teaspoon salt	1 cup milk

Preheat the oven to 400F (205C). Spray 12 muffin cups with nonstick cooking spray.

In a medium bowl, mix together the flour and salt.

In a small bowl, beat the eggs until light and beat in the milk. Add the liquid ingredients to the dry ingredients and stir until mixed but not overblended.

Pour the batter into the prepared muffin pans. Place in hot oven immediately and bake 20 minutes (without looking!), then reduce the oven temperature to 350F (175C) and bake an additional 15 minutes. Check popovers—the tops should have ballooned up and turned golden brown; bake another 5 minutes if needed. Serve at once.

Variations

Add a little protein and calcium by adding 1 tablespoon of grated hard cheese, such as Cheddar, Gruyère or Parmesan to each popover. Spoon half the batter into the muffin cups, sprinkle on the cheese, and cover with the remaining batter.

For an Indian flavor, add 1/2 teaspoon curry powder to the batter. Or stir a minced garlic clove into the batter.

Classic popover recipes use melted butter. If you feel like indulging, put a pat of butter into each muffin cup and melt in the preheated oven. Then pour in the batter and bake.

Southern Spoon Bread

If you've never tasted spoon bread, I suggest you make this dish for your very next breakfast. A cross between corn bread and a soufflé, spoon bread is the perfect partner for egg dishes. Or serve it as a main dish, topped with fresh fruit and yogurt.

MAKES ABOUT 8 SERVINGS.

5 eggs, separated	1 cup yellow cornmeal
1/8 teaspoon cream of tartar	1 teaspoon salt
1 to 2 tablespoons sugar	3 tablespoons butter or margarine,
3 1/4 cups whole milk	cut into pieces

Preheat oven to 375F (190C). Spray a nonstick 2-quart soufflé or casserole dish with non-stick cooking spray.

In a small bowl, beat the egg whites and cream of tartar until the whites are stiff but not dry. Set aside.

In a large bowl, with same beater, beat the egg yolks until light and stir in the sugar. Set aside.

In a large saucepan, bring the milk to a boil over medium heat, then turn the heat down so the mixture simmers. Stirring constantly, slowly add the cornmeal and salt. Add the butter or margarine and cook, stirring constantly, 1 to 2 minutes, until the mixture thickens. Remove from the heat.

A spoonful at a time, whisk the cornmeal mixture into the egg yolks. Finally fold in the beaten egg whites. Pour the mixture into the prepared dish.

Place in the oven immediately. Bake 40 to 45 minutes or until puffed and golden brown, and when a knife is inserted off-center, the knife comes out clean. (Allow to cook at least 30 minutes before peeking.) Serve at once with a spoon.

Variation

Prepare as above, but use 8 individual soufflé dishes. Reduce cooking time to 30 to 35 minutes.

Brown Soda Bread

When you rise at an Irish country house and come down to breakfast, you'll be offered a choice of breads: the white kind with currants or the brown kind, below. This one has a wonderful grainy texture.

MAKES 1 LOAF.

2 cups whole-wheat flour
1 cup all-purpose flour
1/4 cup sugar (optional)
2 tablespoons wheat germ
1 1/2 teaspoons baking soda

1/2 teaspoon baking powder
1 teaspoon salt
1 3/4 cups buttermilk
1/4 cup vegetable oil

Preheat the oven to 400F (205C). Spray a nonstick baking sheet with nonstick cooking spray.

In a large bowl, mix together the flours, sugar, if using, wheat germ, baking soda, baking powder, and salt.

In a large measuring cup, stir together the buttermilk and oil. Add the buttermilk mixture to the dry ingredients and stir briefly until just combined.

With your hands, shape the dough into a large ball, place it on the baking sheet and press lightly on the top so that the dough forms a domed round shape. With a sharp knife, cut an X on the top of the bread.

Bake 40 minutes or until lightly browned. Turn onto a wire rack and cool.

Mrs. Flanagan's Irish Soda Bread

Mrs. Flanagan is my mom and she's only Irish by marriage. She's lived in Ireland for years though, and is a great cook. Here's her recipe for the best soda bread you'll ever taste.

MAKES 1 LOAF.

2 cups all-purpose flour
1 tablespoon sugar (optional)
1 1/2 teaspoons baking powder
1/4 teaspoon baking soda
1/2 teaspoon salt

1 teaspoon caraway seeds
1/2 cup currants (optional)
1 cup buttermilk
2 tablespoons vegetable oil

Preheat the oven to 350F (175C). Spray a nonstick baking sheet with nonstick baking spray.

In a large bowl, mix together the flour, sugar, if using, baking powder, baking soda, salt, and caraway seeds. Mix in the currants, if using.

In a large measuring cup, stir together the buttermilk and oil. Pour the buttermilk mixture into the dry ingredients and stir just enough to combine.

With your hands, shape the dough into an oval shape and place it on the prepared baking sheet. Let the dough rest 5 minutes before putting it in the oven.

Bake about 40 minutes or until bread springs back when pressed with your finger. Turn onto a wire rack and cool.

Cereal

Packaged cereal, swimming in milk, is undoubtedly America's favorite breakfast. And why not? A bowl of cereal with milk and a glass of juice is a pretty decent start, nutritionally, to the day. Besides, breakfast cereal is as American as spacious skies and amber waves of grain.

A Short History of Cereal

If you think the health-food fad began in the 1960s, guess again. It all began in the early 1800s, when a handful of Protestant reformers did their best to transform the way people ate. Sylvester Graham (of Graham flour fame), toured the country preaching the virtues of cold showers, sexual abstinence, and a healthy diet of fresh fruit and whole grains. Ellen White, founding mother of Seventh Day Adventism, had visions that told her to give up meat and eat simple foods. Finally, Ellen White's disciple, John Harvey Kellog, invented the corn flake (in—where else?—Battle Creek, Michigan), and the rest is cereal history.

By the turn of the century, cereal was big business and the major manufacturers were slugging it out on the billboards. At Quaker Oats, a new machine was developed that puffed rice. "The Food That's Shot From Guns" debuted at the 1904 St. Louis World's Fair. Charles W. Post was busy, too, introducing the blood-reddening, nerve-steadying Grape-

Nuts in 1897 and the renowned "Elijaha's Manna" cereal, Post Toasties, in 1907. Wheaties, a General Mills product, was on the market nine years before the company decided it needed a slogan to run on a baseball park billboard, thus giving birth to the "breakfast of champions."

But that was nothing compared to the enormous marketing effort that goes into selling you breakfast cereal today. All you have to do is look at the amount of space cereal takes up in your local grocery store to see what an important role it plays in American breakfasts.

The Right Stuff

If it was hard choosing between cereal shot from guns and the breakfast of champions at the turn of the century, it certainly hasn't gotten any easier for the modern consumer, standing in the cereal aisle comparing the RDAs of various products. Here's what to look for:

Fat   Look for a low-fat cereal and watch out for packaged granolas, which tend to be fat laden. Less than 2 grams of fat per serving is ideal.

Fiber   Cereal is the perfect place to find your daily allotment of fiber. In general, the more whole grains there are in the cereal, the higher the fiber content. Check under "carbohydrate information" on the label to find out how many grams of fiber you'll get in a serving of cereal. As a rule, you'll find the most fiber in "bran" cereals, the least in rice cereals. Look for a mixture of soluble and insoluble fibers.

Iron   Look for a cereal that meets at least 30 percent of your Recommended Daily Allowance of iron, especially if you are a vegetarian. Try to drink a glass of orange juice with your cereal; it will help your body absorb the iron.

Sugar   Avoid cereals with more than 5 grams of sugar per serving. Even cereals that aren't marketed as "frosted" or otherwise sugar-coated may contain high levels of sweetener. Don't be taken in by "maple-" or "honey"-flavored cereal. Sugar is sugar, regardless of the form it takes. Likewise be aware that a manufacturer may use several different kinds of sweeteners. Not surprisingly, the cereals that manufacturers oversweeten tend to be low on fiber and other good ingredients.

Vitamins   These are among the "good" additives; a fortified cereal that meets at least 25 percent of your RDAs is a good bet.

Packaged Cereals

If packaged cereal is a staple at your breakfast table, try to vary the cereals you eat. Some cereals offer more fiber, others more iron, and so on, so if you mix it up you'll get more benefit in the long run. (You might take this idea a bit further and use the "mad scientist" approach, mixing together several cereals at a single serving.)

Home-Prepared Cold Cereals

With all the cereals on the market, is there any point in making your own? In a few cases the answer is yes. There isn't much point in buying your own "gun" to make puffed wheat, but there's a lot to be said for preparing your own granola and muesli. You can tailor-make these cereals to meet your personal taste and you can control the fat and sugar content.

Hot Cereals

Hot cereals deserve a revival. They're easy to cook, tasty, and nutritious, and, as the saying goes, they stick to your ribs. Hot cereals are abundantly available in slow-, fast-, and instant-cooking variations.

Buy your favorite oatmeal or rice or wheat cereal and make it according to the package directions. At the last minute, stir in one or more of these ingredients (amounts are based on 2 cups cooked cereal).

Dairy Products　Add 1/2 cup buttermilk, plain yogurt, cottage cheese, or ricotta cheese.

Flavorings　Add pinches of nutmeg, allspice, cinnamon, and ginger. Stir in 1/2 teaspoon vanilla or almond extract.

Nuts and Fruits　Stir in 2 tablespoons chopped pecans or walnuts and/or 2 tablespoons raisins or 2 tablespoons dried or 1/4 cup fresh chopped fruit, such as bananas, apples, or pears. Or stir in 1/2 cup applesauce or 2 tablespoons peanut butter.

If you've never tried hominy grits—a staple on Southern breakfast tables—find out about this excellent savory side dish. Serve grits with red-eye gravy if that's your fancy; otherwise, see the variations on pages 76–77.

Basic Granola

There are hundreds of ways to make granola, depending on your personal preferences (sesame seeds versus pumpkin seeds, honey versus brown sugar). Here's a basic recipe; see the variations and tailor-make your own version.

MAKES ABOUT 5 CUPS.

2 cups old-fashioned rolled oats

1/2 cup wheat germ

1 cup coarsely chopped nuts (walnuts, cashews, pecans, almonds)

1 cup mixed seeds (pumpkin, sunflower, sesame)

1/2 cup raisins

1/3 cup vegetable oil

1/3 cup honey

1 teaspoon pure vanilla extract

Preheat oven to 325F (165C). In a large roasting pan, thoroughly mix the oats, wheat germ, nuts, seeds, and raisins.

In a large measuring cup, mix together oil, honey, and vanilla. Pour oil mixture over the oat mixture and stir well. Bake 30 to 45 minutes or until golden, stirring every 10 minutes.

Let the granola cool, then store it in an airtight container in the refrigerator up to 4 weeks.

Variations

To the oat mixture, add any of the following: 1/2 cup shredded coconut; 1/2 cup dried banana chips; 1/2 cup chopped dried fruits such as apple, date, fig, etc.; 1/2 teaspoon ground cinnamon, 1 cup of your favorite flaked cereal.

Instead of honey, stir in the same amount of brown sugar or maple syrup. As you add to the amount of dry ingredients, you should increase the amount of oil and sweetener: add 1 tablespoon of each for every 1 cup of dry ingredients.

In place of 1/2 cup of oats, you can use whole-wheat, barley, or soy flour.

Hidden Meadow Granola

This granola, served at Hidden Meadow Bed and Breakfast in Lyme, Connecticut, tastes great and is full of protein and calcium.

MAKES ABOUT 6 CUPS.

2 1/2 cups old-fashioned rolled oats
1/2 cup nonfat dried milk powder
  (not instant)
1/2 cup soy flour
1/2 cup wheat germ
1/2 cup sesame seeds

1/2 cup sunflower kernels
1/2 cup unsweetened shredded dried
  coconut
1/2 cup chopped walnuts (optional)
1/2 cup vegetable oil
1/2 cup honey

Preheat oven to 275F (135C). In a large roasting pan, combine oats, milk powder, soy flour, wheat germ, sesame seeds, sunflower kernels, coconut, and walnuts, if using.

In a large measuring cup, combine oil and honey. Pour oil mixture over the oat mixture and stir well. Bake about 45 minutes, stirring twice, or until the mixture is lightly browned. Be careful not to burn it.

Spoon mixture immediately into a large airtight container and store in the refrigerator up to 2 weeks.

Muesli

Muesli is the invention of Dr. Bircher-Benner, a Swiss physician who was part of the health reform movement of the late nineteenth century. The ingredients are similar to those of granola, but, without sweeteners or fats, it's a simpler dish. Like granola, muesli is open to interpretation, so play around with this recipe and add other ingredients of your choice.

MAKES ABOUT 5 CUPS.

3 cups rolled oats
1/2 cup raisins or currants
1/2 cup wheat germ
1/2 to 1 cup dried fruits: chopped apricots,
    dates, figs, apples, pears, etc.

1/2 to 1 cup nuts: almond slices or
    chopped walnuts, pecans, hazelnuts, etc.

Mix together all the ingredients and store in an airtight container for up to 4 weeks.

To serve, pour milk on the muesli, mix it into yogurt, or try adding your favorite fruit juice instead of milk. For a warm cereal, serve with steamed or heated milk.

Variations

Omit the dried fruits; instead, serve the muesli with diced fresh apple, pear, and banana.

For a crisper, less raw-tasting variation, spread muesli on a baking sheet and bake 15 to 20 minutes in a preheated 350F (175C) oven, stirring every 5 minutes.

Cheesy Hominy Grits

This traditional Southern side dish is right in keeping with the new emphasis on grains. You don't need to serve grits with eggs. Team this recipe with a fruit salad and a glass of skim milk, and you've got a tasty and nutritious meal.

MAKES ABOUT 6 SERVINGS.

2 1/2 cups water
1/2 teaspoon salt
1/2 cup hominy grits

3/4 cup grated low-fat hard cheese:
      Monterey Jack, Cheddar, etc.

In a medium saucepan, bring water and salt to a boil. Stir in grits and then reduce heat to medium-low. Cook 12 to 15 minutes, stirring occasionally. Add cheese, cover pot, and remove from stove. Let stand 2 minutes, then stir and serve.

Variation

For a more exotic variation, stir in crumbled goat cheese, feta cheese, or cream cheese.

Mary Jones's Salsa Grits

Most folk serve grits with butter or cheese. Here's a low-fat variation from a North Carolina gal.

MAKES ABOUT 6 SERVINGS.

2 1/4 cups water
1/2 teaspoon salt
1/2 cup hominy grits
1 ear corn on the cob, kernels cut
    from cob

3/4 cup salsa
1/4 cup sliced pitted ripe olives (optional)
2 tablespoons chopped fresh cilantro

In a medium saucepan, bring water and salt to a boil. Stir in grits and then reduce heat to medium-low. Cook 10 minutes, stirring occasionally. Add corn, salsa, and olives, if using, and cook 3 to 5 minutes.

    Garnish with fresh cilantro.

Hot off the Griddle

Great news: those perennial breakfast favorites, pancakes, waffles, and French toast can still be enjoyed without interference from the nutrition police. Unlike their disgraced cousins, egg and meat dishes, this great triumvirate still reigns supreme at the breakfast table thanks to its high-fiber, low-fat profile.

There is however one proviso. Instead of slathering your pancakes (or French toast or waffles) with butter and maple syrup, let their great natural flavor speak for itself. Fresh fruit makes an excellent partner for a breakfast from the griddle. Try any of the toppings on pages 89 to 97 for some tasty alternatives to syrup, or spread on some fruit-sweetened jam.

None of these foods takes long to cook, especially if you make some preparations the night before. Since waffle and pancake recipes generally include some rising agents (like baking powder), it's best to mix up the dry and liquid ingredients separately and store the latter in the refrigerator. In the morning, just heat the griddle and while it's warming, mix together your two sets of ingredients. (Having said that, I can also report that I've frequently used leftover batter the next day and find that even batters that rely on delicate ingredients like beaten egg white hold up pretty well.)

Please refer to "A Word About Ingredients" on pages 7 to 9. In addition to cutting back on the fats and cholesterol in recipes, you can reduce your fat consumption still further by using a nonstick griddle, frying pan, or waffle iron and a nonstick cooking spray instead of butter or margarine.

Storing and Serving Pancakes, Waffles and French Toast

There's no question that the ideal time to eat a pancake (or waffle or piece of French toast) is about thirty seconds after it leaves the griddle. The problem with this is that it makes it awfully hard for the chef to sit down and eat with his or her family and guests. It is not necessarily unpleasant to stand at the griddle passing out pancakes, especially if your breakfast table is in the kitchen and if other family members are willing to spell you while you sit down and eat.

If you prefer to eat together, though, just heat your oven to 250F (120C) before you get started and put in a baking sheet. As you make the pancakes—or waffles or French toast slices—put them in the oven on the warm baking sheet until you have cooked enough for everyone. (You might have a hot topping like Black Friar Fruit Sauce, page 94, warming on the back burner to ensure that each bite is warm and moist.)

Or to save time in the morning you can make pancakes, waffles, or French toast the night before. Let them cool and then wrap each one individually in foil. In the morning, place the pancake, waffle, or slice of French toast directly on a clean rack in a preheated 350F (175C) oven.

About Cooking Pancakes

My mother always says that the first pancake in every batch needs to be tossed out. I think she has a point. It has to do, I think, with getting the temperature of the griddle just right, something you get the rhythm of as you work.

The griddle (or frying pan) needs to be hot but not too hot—more like medium-hot—and you need to give the nonstick cooking spray time to get hot, too. There's no hurry because another of Mom's rules is to always let your batter sit at room temperature for a couple of minutes before you start cooking.

A ladle, not your mixing spoon, is the best instrument for pouring out the batter onto the griddle and about 4 or 5 inches in diameter is an ideal, easy-to-flip size for pancakes. (Many people, especially small children, enjoy smaller "silver dollar" pancakes.)

As the pancake cooks, small circular crevasses, like the craters on the moon, spread across the surface of the pancake. When to flip is a matter of gauging the number of craters and gently checking the underside of the pancake with your spatula to see if it's lightly browned and firm. A flick of the wrist and you're in the clear.

Some people like to press down on the flipped pancake with the back of the spatula to hasten the cooking, whereas others feel this interferes with the rising process, and still others avoid this proceeding because they like their pancakes slightly damp and gloppy in the middle. Whatever your style, don't cook the pancake much longer after flipping; this side will be ready much sooner than the first. Serve the pancake as soon as the bottom is pleasantly browned. (If you're one of those damp and gloppy fans, bear in mind that you want the potentially salmonella-carrying egg to be thoroughly cooked.) Only flip the pancake once; it's not a hamburger.

About Waffles

If you want to dress up your breakfasts, a waffle iron is the best investment you can make. If there are no small children about, put the waffle iron right on the breakfast table and cook the waffles on site. By all means shop for a nonstick waffle iron. You'll use less fat in cooking and cleanup is a breeze. You might look around for a novelty iron, such as a heart-shaped one or one that offers various surfaces. A Belgian waffle iron will make pleasingly deep waffles; however, waffle recipes generally work on all sizes and shapes of waffle iron.

Waffle recipes tend to call for a little more oil than pancake recipes. On the other hand, if your iron is properly conditioned (see the manufacturer's instructions), it will need no extra oil for cooking. (To convert a pancake recipe to a waffle recipe, simply add oil—about 1/4 cup to every 4 cups batter.)

When your waffle iron is nice and hot, ladle some batter into the center of the iron and close the iron. The batter will spread to the edges of the iron. If it doesn't reach the edges this time, use a little more next time. In a little while, steam will start escaping from the sides of the iron. When the steam stops, the waffle is about ready. Open cautiously and see how it looks—it should be a beautiful golden brown.

Since I don't know how big your waffle iron is, the estimated yields in the recipes that follow are meant only as very rough guidelines.

About French Toast

There's a telling scene at the beginning of the film *Kramer vs. Kramer* in which Dustin Hoffman, the newly single parent, tries to make French toast by cramming a piece of bread into a coffee mug full of beaten egg while his son complains that he's not doing it the "right" way. Toward the end of the film, when we think Hoffman's son is going to go live with his mother, there's a scene in which father and son make one last piece of French toast together, the right way, as Hoffman has learned to do. The unspoken message is that Hoffman has evolved as a parent and now knows how to care for his child properly.

French toast (or "eggy bread," as the English call it) may be the ultimate comfort food. Chewy, a little on the bland side, made of the humblest ingredients—bread and egg—it warms and satisfies.

One element crucial to the success of your French toast is the quality of your bread. By all means use a whole-wheat bread to boost your family's fiber intake. Ordinary sliced bread has a certain comfort factor, but delicious specialty breads make spectacular French toast. Challah makes especially good French toast, or try raisin-cinnamon bread. Whatever kind of bread you use, day-old or slightly stale bread has the best texture for making French toast.

Use a deep-sided plate to mix up your batter. Place your first piece of bread in the batter, give it a few seconds to soak up the batter, then turn and coat the other side. Fry the French toast as you would a pancake.

Baked French toast is an easy alternative to standing at the stove frying individual slices. Simply spray a nonstick roasting pan with nonstick spray, spread a layer of bread on the bottom of the pan and pour French toast batter (see page 84) over the bread. Bake at 400F (205C) about 30 minutes or until the toast is golden brown.

There are many more elaborate recipes for baked (or "stuffed") French toast. I've included one in this chapter but I've saved most of them for the Sweet Treats chapter (pages 151 to 161).

Basic Pancakes

If you like your pancakes plain and simple, here's a very straightforward recipe.

MAKES 12 TO 15 PANCAKES.

1 1/2 cups all-purpose flour

2 tablespoons sugar

1 teaspoon baking powder

1/2 teaspoon baking soda

1/2 teaspoon salt

1 1/2 cups milk

2 eggs, beaten

2 tablespoons vegetable oil

In a large bowl, mix together the flour, sugar, baking powder, baking soda, and salt.

In a 4-cup measuring cup, mix the remaining ingredients and add the contents of the measuring cup to the larger bowl. Mix until dry ingredients are just moistened.

Cook pancakes on a hot griddle over medium-high heat, following the instructions on page 66.

Variations

There are as many variations on this theme as you can think of: stir in 1/2 cup fresh or frozen berries; 1/4 cup finely chopped nuts; 1/2 cup diced apple or pear, with a sprinkling of cinnamon and nutmeg; 1/3 cup raisins or currants; 4 bacon slices, cooked crispy and crumbled; 1/4 cup sunflower or pumpkin seeds; or replace half the milk with applesauce.

Pear-Granola Pancakes

Here's a pancake with added crunch and a delightful flavor.

MAKES ABOUT 16 TO 20 PANCAKES.

1 cup Basic Granola (page 59)

1 recipe Basic Pancakes (page 69)

1 medium pear, shredded

In a large bowl, mash the granola gently with a potato masher just enough to break up any big clumps.

Prepare pancake batter as directed. Add the granola and pear to the batter and stir just until blended.

Cook pancakes on a hot griddle over medium-high heat, following the instructions on page 66.

Lemon-Ricotta Pancakes

This sublime pancake recipe comes from former innkeeper Julie Lowell, of Great Barrington, Massachusetts. The pancakes have a light, delicate flavor that's just a little like cheesecake. Serve them with fresh sliced strawberries or fruit-sweetened jam.

MAKES 6 TO 8 PANCAKES.

3 eggs, separated
1/4 cup all-purpose flour
1/4 cup vegetable oil
3/4 cup ricotta cheese

2 tablespoons sugar
1/4 teaspoon salt
1 tablespoon grated lemon zest or
   1/4 teaspoon lemon extract

In a small bowl, beat the egg whites until they hold stiff peaks. Set aside.

In a larger bowl, use the same beater to beat together the egg yolks, flour, oil, ricotta cheese, sugar, salt, and lemon zest or extract. Fold in the beaten egg whites gently but thoroughly until there are no white streaks.

Because of their composition, ricotta pancakes are slightly more delicate than standard flour-based recipes. Pour about 3 tablespoons of batter per pancake onto a hot griddle over medium-high heat. Cook about 1 1/2 minutes before checking the underside to make sure it is nicely browned and the pancake is sturdy enough to flip. After flipping, cook about 1 minute before removing from the pan.

You can keep the pancakes in the oven at 250F (120C) until ready to serve, but don't try to reheat later.

Note

To make ricotta cheese easier to measure, first pour the oil into your measuring cup and then add ricotta cheese until the oil reaches the 1-cup line.

Cornmeal Pancakes

Crispy pancakes with a down-home flavor—easy and delicious!

MAKES 12 TO 15 PANCAKES.

1 cup all-purpose flour
1/2 cup cornmeal
2 teaspoons baking powder
1/2 teaspoon salt

1/2 teaspoon baking soda
2 eggs
1 1/2 cups milk
1/4 cup vegetable oil

In a large bowl, combine flour, cornmeal, baking powder, salt, and baking soda.

In a medium bowl, beat the eggs and beat in the milk and oil. Add liquid ingredients to the dry ingredients and mix until just blended.

Cook pancakes on a hot griddle over medium-high heat, following the instructions on page 66.

Variations

For a less grainy pancake, adjust the ratio of flour to cornmeal to suit your taste. You may want to crumble in a couple of strips of crispy, drained bacon or 1/4 cup diced cooked turkey or ham. Or add 1/2 cup drained cooked corn kernels.

Orange Buttermilk Pancakes

The fragrant aroma of these tasty pancakes will lure even sleepy-heads out of bed and to the breakfast table.

MAKES 15 TO 18 PANCAKES.

1 1/2 cups all-purpose flour
2 tablespoons sugar
1 teaspoon baking powder
1/2 teaspoon baking soda
1/2 teaspoon salt
2 eggs

2 tablespoons vegetable oil
1 1/4 cups buttermilk
1/4 cup fresh orange juice
2 tablespoons grated orange zest
1 tablespoon grated lemon zest

In a large bowl, mix the flour, sugar, baking powder, baking soda, and salt.

In a medium bowl, beat the eggs and stir in oil, buttermilk, orange juice, orange zest, and lemon zest. Add liquid ingredients to the dry ingredients and mix until just blended.

Cook pancakes on a hot griddle over medium-high heat, following the instructions on page 66.

Risen Pancakes

By taking a little extra trouble—and by making your batter the night before—you can make the perfect pancake. This recipe calls for yeast, which makes the pancakes light and fluffy.

MAKES ABOUT 16 TO 20 PANCAKES.

1 1/4 teaspoons active dry yeast
3 1/2 teaspoons sugar
2 tablespoons lukewarm water
3 eggs, separated
2 cups buttermilk
1/2 teaspoon baking soda

1/4 teaspoon salt
2 tablespoons vegetable oil
1 3/4 cups all-purpose flour
1/2 teaspoon baking powder
1/4 teaspoon ground cinnamon (optional)

In a small bowl, sprinkle yeast and sugar into lukewarm water and stir gently. Let stand until bubbling, about 5 minutes.

In another small bowl, beat the egg whites until stiff but not dry.

In a large bowl, combine egg yolks, buttermilk, baking soda, salt, and oil. Beat with an electric mixer on low until thoroughly mixed. Add the yeast mixture and beat 1 minute.

In a medium bowl, mix together the flour, baking powder, and cinnamon, if using. Add dry ingredients to the liquid ingredients and beat just until the ingredients are combined. Add the egg whites and fold them into the batter with a spoon. Cover and refrigerate the batter overnight.

Take the batter out of the refrigerator 10 to 15 minutes before you use it. Cook pancakes on a hot griddle over medium-high heat, following the instructions on page 66.

Edgecombe-Coles Apple Dutch Babies

Oven-baked Dutch Babies are a wonderful alternative to stovetop pancakes. From the Edgecombe-Coles House in Camden, Maine, this recipe puffs up beautifully.

MAKES 4 SERVINGS.

2 medium apples, cored and sliced (not peeled)
1 to 2 tablespoons brown sugar
1/2 teaspoon ground cinnamon

1 cup milk
4 eggs
1 cup all-purpose flour
2 teaspoons butter or margarine

Preheat oven to 400F (205C). In a large nonstick frying pan, cook apples, sugar, and cinnamon over medium-low heat until the apples are soft and a sauce forms. Set aside.

Put the milk and eggs in a blender and process at high speed until mixed. With the blender still operating at high, gradually add flour until the mixture is smooth. Set aside.

Put the butter or margarine in a 10-inch cast-iron or other nonstick ovenproof skillet and put the skillet in the oven. When the butter or margarine starts to brown, remove the pan from the oven, pour in the batter, and then spoon the apple mixture on top of the batter.

Bake 30 minutes or until puffed and browned. Cut into 4 wedges and serve immediately.

Variations

You can substitute similar quantities of pear, berries, crushed pineapple, peaches, plums, and other fruits for the apples. Alternatively, Dutch Babies can be prepared without fruit and served with maple syrup or other toppings.

Three-Berry Clafouti

Like Dutch Babies, clafoutis are a form of oven-baked pancake. But whereas Dutch Babies preserve the basic consistency of pancakes, clafoutis, which have a greater ratio of egg-milk mixture to flour, are more like a dense soufflé or pudding. The clafouti will rise impressively and present beautifully as a company dish.

MAKES 4 SERVINGS.

3 eggs (no substitutes)
1 1/4 cups low-fat or whole milk
3/4 cup all-purpose flour
1/4 cup sugar
1 1/2 teaspoons pure vanilla extract

1/4 teaspoon ground nutmeg
1/8 teaspoon salt
1 1/8 cups mixed berries: blackberries, raspberries, and blueberries

Preheat the oven to 350F (175C). Spray a 9-inch nonstick pie plate with nonstick cooking spray.

In a medium bowl, beat eggs with an electric mixer until light. Turn mixer speed to low and continue beating as you add milk and then flour, sugar, vanilla, nutmeg, and salt. Pour the batter into the prepared pie plate. Sprinkle 1 cup of the berries on top of the batter.

Place in hot oven immediately and bake 45 minutes or until a knife comes out clean.

Serve hot or warm, with remaining 1/8 cup berries sprinkled on top.

Crepes

A crepe is a thin pancake. You can turn any pancake recipe into a crepe recipe by increasing the ratio of milk to flour and eliminating the leavening agents.

MAKES ABOUT 18 (6-INCH) CREPES.

2 eggs
1 1/2 cups milk
1 cup all-purpose flour

1/2 teaspoon salt
2 tablespoons butter or margarine, melted
1/3 cup fruit-sweetened jam

In a large bowl, beat the eggs until light. Beat in the milk.

In a medium bowl, combine the flour and salt. Add dry ingredients to the liquid ingredients and beat just until ingredients are combined. Let the batter stand in the refrigerator 2 1/2 hours. Stir in the melted butter or margarine.

Cooking a crepe is a bit trickier than cooking a pancake. Use a nonstick pan, preferably a 6-inch crepe or omelette pan, but you can use an ordinary nonstick frying pan. Spray the pan with nonstick cooking spray. Heat 1 to 2 minutes over medium-high heat, then ladle in about 2 tablespoons of batter and swirl to thinly coat the bottom of the pan. Cook about 1 minute, holding onto the handle of the pan and keeping up a gentle swirling motion as the crepe cooks. Flip the crepe, cook a few seconds, and then remove crepe to a dish. Repeat with remaining batter.

Spread jam on each crepe and then roll the crepe, jelly-roll style, around it.

Variation

For a more complex but rewarding variation, flip the crepe and immediately spoon a line of filling down the middle. Flip the sides of the crepe back around the filling, cook 2 to 4 minutes longer, and then serve.

Suggested fillings for one crepe: try 1 tablespoon of thinly sliced banana with a sprinkling of brown sugar; 1 tablespoon of ham, cut in thin strips, with a tablespoon of grated Swiss cheese; or 2 tablespoons minced smoked salmon with 1 teaspoon crème fraîche and a sprinkling of minced fresh dill.

Basic Blintzes

If you've ruled out blintzes in the past because of their creamy fillings, think again. The new fat-free cheeses make it possible to enjoy this memorable dish again. Top with a fruit salad or other topping from the topping chapter.

MAKES 18 BLINTZES.

Crepes (page 77)
1 1/2 cups cottage cheese
3/4 cup cream cheese or Mock Cream
   Cheese (page 90)

1 tablespoon sugar (optional)
1/2 teaspoon pure vanilla extract

Preheat oven to 350F (175C). Spray a large nonstick baking dish with nonstick cooking spray.

Prepare 18 crepes according to recipe on page 77. Make a stack of finished crepes, putting a sheet of waxed paper between each crepe to keep them from sticking together.

In a medium bowl, combine the cottage cheese, cream cheese or yogurt cheese, and sugar, if using.

Spoon about 1 tablespoon of filling onto each crepe and then fold up the sides and roll into an egg-roll shape. Place them seam side down in the baking dish. (You may now refrigerate the blintzes overnight. If you do, bring them to room temperature on the kitchen counter before heating.)

Bake 10 to 15 minutes, until heated through. Serve hot or warm.

Basic Waffles

Here's how to make the perfect waffle.

MAKES ABOUT 6 WAFFLES.

1 1/2 cups all-purpose flour	1/2 teaspoon salt
1 tablespoon sugar	2 eggs
2 teaspoons baking powder	1 1/2 cups milk
1/2 teaspoon baking soda	1/4 cup vegetable oil

In a large bowl, mix together the flour, sugar, baking powder, baking soda, and salt.

In a smaller bowl, beat the eggs until light and beat in the milk and oil. Add the contents of this bowl to the dry ingredients and mix just until blended.

Bake waffles in a preheated waffle iron according to instructions on page 67.

Variations

Try any of the variations recommended on page 69 for pancakes.

Gingerbread Waffles

If you like gingerbread, you'll love these springy, aromatic waffles. The brown sugar and molasses provide all the sweetener you'll need; top with fresh fruit and yogurt or sour cream.

MAKES ABOUT 6 WAFFLES.

1 egg, separated

1/3 cup packed brown sugar

1 1/4 cups buttermilk

1/4 cup molasses

1/4 cup vegetable oil

1 1/2 cups all-purpose flour

2 teaspoons baking powder

1/2 teaspoon baking soda

1/2 teaspoon salt

1 teaspoon ground ginger

1 teaspoon ground cinnamon

1 teaspoon ground allspice

In a small bowl, beat egg white until stiff but not dry. Set aside.

In a large bowl, beat together the egg yolk, brown sugar, buttermilk, molasses, and oil.

In a medium bowl, combine flour, baking powder, baking soda, salt, ginger, cinnamon, and allspice. Add dry ingredients to liquid ingredients and mix until blended. Fold in beaten egg white.

Bake waffles in a preheated waffle iron according to instructions on page 67.

Molly Stark Blueberry Belgian Buttermilk Waffles

This is one of the most often requested dishes at the Molly Stark Inn in Bennington, Vermont, where the waffles are served with warm Vermont maple syrup. When you try them, I think you'll see why they're so popular.

MAKES 6 TO 8 WAFFLES.

2 cups all-purpose flour

1/4 cup sugar

1 tablespoon baking powder

1 teaspoon baking soda

1/2 teaspoon salt

1 teaspoon ground cinnamon (optional)

3 eggs, separated

1 teaspoon pure vanilla extract

1/3 cup butter or margarine, melted

1 1/2 cups buttermilk

1 cup frozen blueberries (see Note below)

In a large bowl, mix together the flour, sugar, baking powder, salt, and cinnamon, if using.

In a medium bowl, mix the egg yolks, vanilla, butter or margarine, and buttermilk. Add liquid ingredients to the dry ingredients and mix just until blended. (Do not overmix.) Sprinkle blueberries on top of batter.

Beat the egg whites until a little stiff and fold them and the blueberries into the batter.

Bake waffles in a preheated waffle iron according to instructions on page 67. Do not undercook.

Note

Do not defrost frozen blueberries, as they will turn the batter gray.

Oatmeal-Apple Waffles

One of these a day should keep the doctor away, not just because of the apple but also because of the high-fiber oats.

MAKES 4 TO 6 WAFFLES.

1 cup old-fashioned rolled oats
1 cup all-purpose flour
1 tablespoon baking powder
1/2 teaspoon baking soda
1/4 teaspoon salt
1/2 teaspoon ground cinnamon
1/4 teaspoon ground nutmeg

2 eggs
1 cup buttermilk
1/2 cup applesauce
1/4 cup vegetable oil
2 tablespoons brown sugar (optional)
1 cup finely shredded apple

In a medium bowl, combine oats, flour, baking powder, baking soda, salt, cinnamon, and nutmeg.

In a large bowl, beat the eggs until light and beat in buttermilk, applesauce, oil, and brown sugar, if using. Stir in the shredded apple.

Add the dry ingredients to the liquid ingredients and mix just to blend ingredients.

Bake waffles in a preheated waffle iron according to instructions on page 67. You may need extra oil to grease the waffle iron.

Walnut Waffles

Here's a waffle with lots of crunch.

MAKES ABOUT 6 WAFFLES.

1 cup all-purpose flour
1/2 cup whole-wheat flour
1 1/2 teaspoons baking powder
1/2 teaspoon baking soda
1/2 teaspoon salt

2 tablespoons brown sugar (optional)
2 cups buttermilk
1/4 cup vegetable oil
3/4 cup finely chopped walnuts
1/2 cup currants

In a large bowl, mix the flours, baking powder, baking soda, salt, and brown sugar, if using.

In a medium bowl, mix the buttermilk and oil. Add liquid ingredients to the dry ingredients and mix just to blend ingredients. Stir in the walnuts and currants.

Bake waffles in a preheated waffle iron according to instructions on page 67.

Basic French Toast

You can stir any of your favorite flavors into this basic batter.

MAKES 6 SLICES FRENCH TOAST.

2 eggs

1/2 cup milk

1/2 teaspoon pure vanilla extract

6 slices bread

In a dish with deep sides, beat the eggs until light and beat in the milk and vanilla. Dip bread slices into the egg mixture to coat.

Cook according to directions on page 68.

Variations

Maple French Toast

Use only 1 egg and add 2 tablespoons maple syrup. Instead of maple syrup, you might use honey or molasses.

Fruity French Toast

Replace half the milk with orange or pineapple juice and add a few drops of orange extract in place of vanilla.

Or add 2 tablespoons almond flakes and use 1/4 teaspoon almond extract instead of vanilla. Stir in 2 tablespoons sesame seeds or finely chopped nuts or orange and/or lemon zest.

French-Toast Waffles

All the fun of waffles without all the measuring.

MAKES 6 WAFFLES.

6 slices bread   Basic French Toast batter (opposite)

While the waffle iron heats up, dip bread into French toast batter. Put the bread into the waffle iron and cook about 3 to 5 minutes, until golden brown.

French-Toast Sandwiches

If you're in a hurry one morning, here's a great all-in-one meal. You can even eat it on the bus!

MAKES 3 SANDWICHES.

Basic French Toast batter (page 84)
6 thick slices bread

2 tablespoons jam
1/2 banana, peeled and sliced

Prepare 6 slices French toast as described on page 68. Spread with jam and sprinkle banana slices on each of three pieces of French toast. Top with remaining pieces.

Variations

Instead of banana, try sliced strawberries or whole, slightly crushed raspberries or diced apple. Spread cream cheese or ricotta cheese instead of jam on the sandwiches.

For a morning-after-Thanksgiving treat, use cranberry sauce instead of jam and pour on a little maple syrup.

Pineapple Upside-Down French Toast

The flavors of pineapple upside-down cake are duplicated in this tasty recipe.

MAKES 6 SLICES.

2 tablespoons margarine or butter

2 tablespoons brown sugar

1/2 teaspoon cinnamon

6 fresh or canned pineapple rings
   (page 17)

6 thick slices Italian bread

Basic French Toast batter (page 84)

Preheat the oven to 400F (205C). Spray a 13 × 9-inch nonstick baking dish with nonstick cooking spray.

In a small saucepan, melt the butter or margarine and stir in the brown sugar and cinnamon. Spread evenly on the bottom of the baking dish. Arrange the pineapple rings on top of the sugar mixture. Place 1 slice of bread on top of each pineapple ring. Pour the French toast batter evenly over the bread.

Bake 30 to 35 minutes or until the top of the bread is evenly browned.

To serve, remove pineapple-bread portions with a spatula and flip onto plate so that pineapple side is up.

Variation

Place one pitted fresh or maraschino cherry in the center of each pineapple ring.

Toppings

If you're watching your weight or are health conscious, you're probably aware that it's not so much the breakfast food itself—the pancake, the bran muffin, the slice of banana bread—that is likely to make you break your vows. It's what you put on it—the butter, the maple syrup, the chocolate sauce, and the whipped cream—that can be your downfall.

So here is a bevy of recipes for toppings that will help you reduce the amount of fat and sugar you add to your breakfast. As you experiment with recipes like Blueberry-Maple Syrup (page 92) you'll find that you appreciate the subtlety of less sugary flavors. Reduced-fat recipes like Mock Cream Cheese (page 90) can revive the spirits of half-starved dieters.

Many of these toppings are delicious when mixed into hot cereal or spooned on top of cold cereal. Use them in a breakfast buffet of cereal, several kinds of fruit toppings and low-fat yogurt.

Mock Cream Cheese

Here's good news for bagel lovers who worry about the fat and calories in cream cheese. Straining yogurt to make mock cream cheese takes a little advance planning, but it isn't hard to do and is worth the effort. By the way, you can use mock cream cheese in place of the real thing in baking or even in a low-calorie version of your favorite cheesecake!

MAKES ABOUT 1 1/3 CUPS.

3 cups low-fat or nonfat plain yogurt

Line a sieve or colander with dampened cheesecloth. Put the sieve or colander into a bowl. Spoon the yogurt into the lined sieve, carefully wrap everything with plastic wrap, and refrigerate overnight. In the morning, discard the liquid that has collected in the bowl and spoon the firm yogurt into a bowl.

Variations

Instead of the cheesecloth-colander approach, you can use a cone-style drip coffee maker. Simply line the cone with a dampened paper filter, position it over the coffee carafe, fill paper with yogurt, cover the top with plastic, and refrigerate as above.

Any flavor you've enjoyed with the "real thing" will taste great in mock cream cheese. Try adding chopped raisins and walnuts to taste, 1/2 teaspoon of garlic powder and 1 tablespoon of fresh chopped herbs or 1 teaspoon of dried fines herbes, finely diced sun-dried tomatoes, sliced olives, finely chopped smoked salmon or dried fruit.

Fake Cream

If your fondest childhood memories include hot steaming bowls of oatmeal smothered in fresh cream, here's a way to have your porridge and eat it, too.

MAKES ABOUT 2/3 CUP.

1/2 cup low-fat ricotta cheese
2 tablespoons low-fat yogurt
2 tablespoons milk

1 teaspoon sugar or honey (optional)
1 drop yellow food coloring (optional)

Put all the ingredients into the food processor or blender; blend until completely smooth. Cover and refrigerate.

Note

Sadly, fake cream isn't wholly successful in tea or coffee. It works wonderfully with hot or cold fruit dishes, though.

Orange Cream-Cheese Spread

This flavorful spread comes from the Governor's Inn in Ludlow, Vermont, where it is combined handsomely with the inn's Orange Nut Bread (page 158).

MAKES ABOUT 1 1/3 CUPS.

1 cup (8 ounces) cream cheese
1/3 navel orange, including peel, cut into
   sections

1 tablespoon powdered sugar (optional)

Put all the ingredients into the blender and process into a chunky spread.

Blueberry-Maple Syrup

Here's a clever way to cut back on the calories in maple syrup. This recipe is great with pancakes, or try stirring it into hot oatmeal.

MAKES ABOUT 1 1/2 CUPS.

1 cup fresh or frozen blueberries   3/4 cup pure maple syrup

In a small saucepan, warm the blueberries and maple syrup until heated through. With a potato masher, gently press on the berries until they begin to burst (but don't mash to a pulp). Serve hot or warm.

Variations

Orange-Pecan Maple Syrup

Combine 1/2 cup maple syrup, 1/4 cup fresh orange juice, and 1/4 cup chopped pecans and heat until warm.

The Inn at Round Barn Raspberry Maple Syrup

Combine 1 cup maple syrup, 2/3 cup raspberries, and 2 tablespoons raspberry jam and heat until warm.

 THE CREATIVE BREAKFAST

Buttonwood Inn Spicy Apple Syrup

Innkeeper Peter Needham serves this syrup with his To-Die-for French Toast (page 156). Even everyday pancakes and waffles will be enhanced by its tangy flavor.

MAKES ABOUT 1 CUP.

1/2 cup applesauce
1/2 cup apple jelly
1/4 teaspoon ground cinnamon

1/8 teaspoon ground cloves
Dash of salt

Combine all the ingredients in a small saucepan and cook over medium heat, stirring constantly, until the jelly melts and the syrup is hot.

Variation

For a less spicy apple syrup, reduce or eliminate the cloves.

Pineapple-Orange Syrup

This naturally sweet topping is a great alternative to too-sweet syrups.

MAKES ABOUT 1 CUP.

1 (8-ounce) can crushed pineapple

1/2 cup fruit-sweetened orange marmalade

Combine the crushed pineapple, including its natural juices, with the marmalade in a small saucepan. Simmer over medium-low heat about 5 minutes, stirring occasionally. Serve hot.

Blanche's Maple Yogurt

This tasty topping is served as part of a breakfast buffet at Blanche's B & B in Franconia, New Hampshire, along with fresh fruit salad, toasted coconut, ground nuts, and granola.

MAKES ABOUT 2 CUPS.

2 cups plain yogurt
2 tablespoons pure maple syrup

2 teaspoons pure vanilla extract

Mix all the ingredients in a small bowl and whisk until thoroughly blended. Refrigerate until ready to use.

Black Friar Fruit Sauce

Invented by innkeeper Perry Risley to go with his stuffed French toast (page 155), this fruit sauce is delicious with pancakes and waffles, too.

MAKES ABOUT 2 CUPS.

1 cup blueberries
1 cup sliced strawberries
1/4 cup sugar

1/4 cup orange juice
1 tablespoon fresh lemon juice

Combine all the ingredients in a medium saucepan. Cook over medium heat about 5 minutes, stirring occasionally. Let the mixture cool a little and then puree in a food processor or blender. When ready to serve, pour the sauce back into the saucepan and heat until warm.

Variation

Instead of pureeing the syrup, leave berries whole and serve the syrup, warm or cold, as a compote.

Banana Butter

Here's a tasty way to reduce the fat in a spoonful of your regular margarine or butter.

MAKES ABOUT 1/2 CUP.

1 ripe banana
2 tablespoons margarine or butter, softened

1 teaspoon honey

In a small bowl, mash the banana with the back of a fork. Stir in the remaining ingredients and blend well. Serve at once.

Variation

Instead of a banana, beat in 1 tablespoon each finely chopped raisins and walnuts, or mix in 1/8 teaspoon grated ginger and 1 tablespoon grated citrus zest.

Strawberry Sorbet

Serve in small scoops as a first course or use as an unexpected foil to hot pancakes or French toast.

MAKES ABOUT 1 1/2 CUPS.

1/2 cup water

1/4 cup sugar

1 cup sliced strawberries

Combine water and sugar in a medium saucepan and bring to a boil. Simmer 5 minutes and then let the syrup cool.

Place the strawberries in the blender, add sugar syrup, and puree until smooth. Pour into a medium shallow baking dish or plastic storage container. Freeze 2 1/2 hours, remove sorbet, and puree in a blender to eliminate ice crystals that may have formed in the freezing process. (You may need to let the sorbet thaw slightly before cutting it into chunks and putting it in the blender.) Pour back into the container and freeze overnight.

To serve, let the sorbet thaw 15 to 20 minutes. Cut into chunks and serve or puree one last time and scoop out servings.

Pineapple Sorbet

Serve in small scoops as a topping for fresh fruit or as a first course. (Sorbet makes great blender drinks, too—see page 37.)

MAKES ABOUT 1 1/2 CUPS.

1/4 cup plus 2 tablespoons water

1/4 cup sugar

1 1/2 cups pineapple juice

Combine water and sugar in a medium saucepan and bring to a boil. Simmer 5 minutes and then let the syrup cool.

Place the pineapple juice in the blender, add the sugar syrup and process until combined. Pour into a medium shallow baking dish or plastic storage container. Freeze 2 1/2 hours, remove sorbet and puree in a blender to eliminate ice crystals that may have formed in the freezing process. (You may need to let the sorbet thaw slightly before cutting it into chunks and putting it in the blender.) Pour back into the container and freeze overnight.

To serve, let the sorbet thaw 15 to 20 minutes. Cut into chunks and serve or puree one last time and scoop out servings.

Mango Sorbet

This icy fruit topping has a beautiful golden color and a great flavor—perfect as a first course or as a topping for crepes or fruit.

MAKES ABOUT 1 1/2 CUPS.

1/2 cup water   2 ripe mangoes, cut into large chunks
1/4 cup sugar

Combine water and sugar in a medium saucepan and bring to a boil. Simmer 5 minutes and then let the syrup cool.

Place the mango in the blender, add sugar syrup and puree until smooth. Pour into a medium shallow baking dish or plastic storage container. Freeze 2 1/2 hours, remove sorbet, and puree in a blender to eliminate ice crystals that may have formed in the freezing process. (You may need to let the sorbet thaw slightly before cutting it into chunks and putting it in the blender.) Pour back into the container and freeze overnight.

To serve, let the sorbet thaw 15 to 20 minutes. Cut into chunks and serve or puree one last time and scoop out servings.

Variation

A Medley of Sorbet

Prepare Mango Sorbet (above), Strawberry Sorbet (opposite), and Pineapple Sorbet (opposite). Serve small scoops of each in a glass dish.

Hint

For an easy sorbet, buy a can of your favorite fruit in heavy syrup. Freeze in the can overnight. In the morning, let the can thaw a bit before opening. Then blend until smooth and transfer into an appropriate container. Freeze 2 1/2 hours, puree again, and refreeze. If you don't want to use fruit packed in heavy syrup, buy fruit packed in light syrup for an icier-textured sorbet.

Eggs

According to ancient Egyptian legend, the god Ptah created the egg out of the sun and the moon. The peoples of the ancient world tended not to eat many eggs, though; they preferred to let them hatch and grow into poultry. No doubt their cholesterol levels were correspondingly low.

An egg yolk contains 213 milligrams of cholesterol—a daunting fact for health-conscious egg-lovers. The easy solution is to substitute two egg whites for every whole egg in your favorite egg recipe. Better yet, make only one whole egg and dress it up with Oven-Baked Hash Browns (page 121), Mixed Grill (page 124), and one of the great breads and muffins in "The Creative Bakery" chapter.

All About Eggs

What's in an Egg?   While they're incredibly pleasing from an aesthetic point of view, brown eggs are identical on the inside to white eggs. Free-range eggs come—theoretically at least—from chickens who've been allowed to run around and peck at one another in an open, traditional barnyard setting rather than having been confined in the harsh environment of the large poultry factories. Connoisseurs swear that free-range eggs taste better, too. Always look for Grade A eggs. If you can't remember which of your eggs are fresh and which hard boiled, stand them on end and spin them. The hard-boiled ones will stay spinning while the fresh ones will flop.

Salmonella and You   Salmonella is a nasty little bacteria that can cause a form of food poisoning called salmonellosis. Symptoms include fever, headache, vomiting, and diarrhea. Salmonella can be present in raw eggs, both in the yolk and the white, but the bacteria is destroyed when eggs are properly cooked. Make sure the cooked white of the egg is completely "white" and set; the yolk should begin to thicken, although it need not harden.

Don't Wash Your Eggs   Apparently some overzealous cooks with time on their hands are in the habit of washing their eggs before refrigerating them. This is not a good idea, not only because it leads to Crazed Cook Syndrome but also because washing eggs may actually introduce bacteria into the egg through osmosis. So next time you're tempted to wash your eggs, sit down and listen to some music instead.

Separate but Equal   When a recipe calls for egg white, it's important that not a speck of yolk or shell pollute the egg white; otherwise, the white won't whip up nicely. Invest in an egg separator from a good kitchen shop; they're more reliable and hygienic than passing the yolk between broken shells.

Classic Egg Dishes

Many egg recipes can be adapted for egg white–only or egg white and whole egg combinations, but some really are best made with the whole egg. Here's a how-to for making classic egg dishes:

   T H E   C R E A T I V E   B R E A K F A S T

Over Easy This is one of the most challenging egg dishes as you must manage to cook the eggs in such a way that: (1) the white is cooked through, (2) the yolk remains soft and runny, and (3) the yolk doesn't break. The first step is to heat your nonstick pan to a high temperature. Add a little margarine, butter, or oil and heat until the fat starts to sizzle. Crack your egg into the center of the pan and immediately turn the heat down to medium-low. With a spatula, check the under-surface of the white. As soon as it appears solid and slightly browned, flip the egg. Wait 10 seconds, check to make sure the new under-surface is cooked through and then serve the egg.

Over Hard Much easier than eggs over easy, hard-cooked fried eggs begin the same way, with an egg broken into hot sizzling fat and then the heat turned down. When the white is firm, flip the egg and let it cook for another minute or so.

Sunny Side Up The trick here is to persuade the white to finish cooking before the yolk hardens. Begin as with eggs over easy, breaking the egg into hot fat and then turning down the heat, but cover the frying pan. This will trap the heat from the pan and cause the top of the egg to cook more rapidly. The egg is done when the clear "white" has turned completely white. (Or cook longer if you like your yolk hard.)

Boiled Eggs One great advantage of boiled eggs is that they eliminate the need to use any fat at all. Problems arise when you drop cold eggs into boiling water (they tend to crack), so I favor this method: Fill a pan with plenty of cold water (more than enough to cover the eggs). Carefully lower each egg to the bottom of the pan and place pan over high heat. Once the water boils, turn it down to a simmer. For soft-boiled eggs, cook for another 3 to 6 minutes (according to your taste); for hard-boiled, cook 10 to 15 minutes.

Eating a boiled egg is an art in itself, especially if you use an egg cup (which I heartily recommend for sheer elegance). Place the egg, thicker side down, in the cup and tap against the top of the egg with a knife. Then use a teaspoon to neatly remove the top (a delicate morsel in itself) and eat spoonfuls direct from the shell. Alternatively, turn the egg on its side in a bowl. Strike the center with your knife and break the egg in half, spooning the contents out into the bowl. Mash it up for a less attractive but arguably tastier result.

Scrambled Eggs Probably the easiest egg dish of all is scrambled eggs. It's also probably the dish that works best with egg substitute or egg whites.

Spray a nonstick pan with nonstick cooking spray and set over medium heat. Meanwhile, beat two eggs (or equivalent) in a small bowl with a little milk (a teaspoon to a tablespoon, to taste). Pour the egg mixture into the hot pan and turn the heat down to low. Wait until the egg starts to set and then drag a wooden spoon through it, edge to edge, a few times. Let the mixture start to set and then repeat the process. Keep doing this until the egg is no longer liquid. (Scrambled eggs are very much a matter of personal preference. Some people stir continuously while the eggs cook for a pureed effect, whereas others stir less frequently for a chunkier texture. Some like them well-done and dry, whereas others prefer them wet and gloppy.) Scrambled eggs can be stretched almost indefinitely by a variety of other ingredients.

Poached Eggs   If you had a carton of a dozen eggs, you could poach each one according to a different set of directions. Here's an excellent method, described by Alain Borel, of L'Auberge Provençale (see his excellent Poached Eggs in a Nest à la Provençale, page 106): In a large, nonreactive pot, bring 2 quarts of water, 2 tablespoons white vinegar, and 1 teaspoon salt to a boil, then turn down to a steady simmer. Crack the eggs, one at a time, into a small bowl and gently pour each egg into the simmering water. Cook 3 minutes and then remove with a slotted spoon. Hold the egg over the simmering water for a few seconds to let excess water drain off. Like boiled eggs, poached eggs need no fat. To poach a yolkless egg, simply separate out the yolk before sliding the white into the simmering water. You may want to combine 2 egg whites and use each in place of 1 whole egg in recipes calling for poached eggs.

Baked Eggs   Also known as "shirred" eggs, this is a very easy but extremely elegant dish that will impress your guests out of all proportion to the work involved. Preheat the oven to 425F (220C). Add about 1/2 teaspoon of oil or butter per egg to individual ramekins or a larger baking dish. If you're using a larger dish, allow about a 3-inch-square space per egg and no more—you need the container to define the size of the baked eggs.

Heat dishes in oven about 5 minutes or until the fat is hot and sizzling. Remove dishes from oven and carefully break eggs into fat, either into the center of individual ramekins or evenly spaced in your larger baking dish. (You can make baked eggs without the yolk simply by using 2 egg whites for every whole egg.) Return dishes to the oven, reduce heat to 350F (175C), and cook another 5 to 10 minutes until the white is set for runny yolks or about 15 minutes until yolk is hard.

Another way to prepare baked eggs is to cook them in ramekins placed in a baking pan containing an inch of water. Bake in a preheated 350F (175C) oven 15 to 25 minutes. This will result in a texture that is more like poached eggs and less like fried eggs.

Omelettes   You could probably write an entire book about how to make omelettes, but apart from the rule "you have to break a few eggs to make one," nothing is hard and fast. The best omelette is a two- or three-egg omelette made in a medium frying pan or omelette pan. Bigger omelettes are more practical if you're feeding several people but they're trickier to get right. (For a gang, I'd suggest one of the frittatas on pages 114–117.) Heat a nonstick frying pan that has been sprayed with nonstick cooking spray over medium heat. Meanwhile, beat 2 eggs with 1 teaspoon of milk, salt and pepper to taste and any other spices you like, such as nutmeg, paprika, or chili powder. Pour the egg mixture into the hot pan and wait for the sides of the eggs to start to harden. With a wooden spoon, gently ease the hardened sides from the edges of the pan toward the center, working your way around the pan. Now sprinkle your filling on one half of the egg mixture. As soon as the underside is firm enough to flip, do so, flipping the side without filling onto the side with filling. Gently press down on the omelette with the back of your spatula. Cook 1 to 2 minutes more.

Use no more than 3 tablespoons of filling for each two-egg omelette; otherwise it will be unwieldy. Some filling can go right into the omelette—grated or soft cheese, sliced ham, caviar, fresh chopped herbs, diced smoked salmon, grated apple, chopped bell peppers— whereas others should be cooked (and drained) ahead of time—sautéed onion or zucchini; wilted spinach, arugula, or other greens; steamed broccoli, etc.

Yolkless omelettes can be very successful; just bear in mind that egg whites are more delicate than the whole egg and will cook faster. Whip the egg whites with a hand beater until they are frothy. Pour the egg whites into the hot pan and use a circular motion to swirl the pan to move the whites around. When the clear liquid egg whites start to whiten, add the filling. When the bottom of the egg whites looks firm enough, flip onto the filling, as described above.

Frittatas   The Italian frittata is a relative newcomer to American breakfast tables. It resembles an omelet but is easier to make. It's a splendid company dish as it looks beautiful and can be expanded to feed more people.

There are several ways to make a frittata but the basic strategy is this: You start by sautéing various vegetables in a stovetop-to-oven pan, preferably one with slanted sides, which will make serving the frittata easier. Then you add a mixture of eggs, cheese, and other ingredients and cook a while longer on top of the stove. To finish it off, you cook the frittata for a few minutes under the broiler.

The ingredients you use determine the texture of the frittata as well as cooking time and other factors. Try the recipes that follow and then experiment with your own variations.

Scrambled Ham and Eggs

You can't go far wrong with scrambled eggs. Here are a few of the best versions. You probably won't need to add any oil or other fat, but you may add a tiny bit.

MAKES 1 TO 2 SERVINGS.

2 tablespoons diced cooked ham
2 eggs
1 to 3 teaspoons milk

1 tablespoon shredded Cheddar or
   Swiss cheese (optional)

Sauté ham in a nonstick frying pan over medium-low heat until hot.

Meanwhile, in a small bowl, beat together the eggs and milk and stir in cheese, if using. Pour egg mixture over ham and scramble according to the directions on pages 101–102.

Variations

The possible variations on the scrambled egg are numberless. Here are a few of my favorites.

Mushroom and Feta Scrambled Eggs

Sauté 1 tablespoon thinly sliced green onion and 2 tablespoons thinly sliced mushrooms in a little oil over medium-low heat about 3 minutes. Crumble 1 to 2 tablespoons feta cheese into egg mixture, add to frying pan, and cook as directed in preceding recipe.

Italian Eggs

Sauté 1 tablespoon diced yellow onion over medium-low heat 2 minutes. Add 1 tablespoon chopped, seeded, and diced tomato, and 1 tablespoon diced green bell pepper and sauté about 3 minutes. To the egg mixture, add 1 tablespoon grated mozzarella, 1 teaspoon finely chopped ripe olive and 1 teaspoon finely chopped fresh basil. Add the egg mixture to the frying pan and cook as directed in preceding recipe.

Bloody Mary Eggs

Use tomato juice instead of milk in the egg mixture and add 1/8 to 1/2 teaspoon hot pepper sauce and 2 tablespoons finely chopped fresh cilantro to the egg mixture. Cook as directed in preceding recipe.

Pesto and Sun-Dried Tomato Eggs

Stir 1 teaspoon pesto into the eggs instead of milk. Pour the eggs into the hot pan and sprinkle in 1 tablespoon minced sun-dried tomatoes. Cook as directed in preceding recipe.

Chile Eggs

Stir 1 teaspoon finely chopped hot chile and 1 tablespoon shredded Monterey Jack cheese into the egg mixture. Cook as directed in preceding recipe. Roll the scrambled eggs up in a tortilla and top with Mock Cream Cheese (page 90) and salsa.

Indian Eggs

Sauté 2 tablespoons finely chopped onion and 1 tablespoon chopped, seeded tomato with a pinch of turmeric, a pinch of cumin, a pinch of ginger, and 1 teaspoon chopped fresh cilantro over medium-low heat 2 to 3 minutes. Stir in egg mixture and cook as directed in preceding recipe. Serve with a dollop of yogurt mixed with chopped fresh cilantro and a pinch of ground ginger.

Poached Eggs in a Nest à la Provençale

This elegant recipe comes from L'Auberge Provençale, a French country-style inn in White Post, Virginia. To my mind it's a substantial meal in itself, but chef Alain Borel tells me he serves it with "sautéed wild mushrooms, pheasant breast, chicken sausage, baked croissant, saffron cottage fries, and a mimosa"!

MAKES 4 SERVINGS.

Salt and pepper to taste
4 thick slices of ripe tomato
2 tablespoons olive oil (plus a few drops)
1/2 cup pine nuts
3 cups chopped fresh spinach
1 cup fresh chicory or dandelion leaves

1 pinch of grated nutmeg
1 teaspoon fresh chopped tarragon
1 teaspoon fresh chopped chives
2 tablespoons vinegar
1 teaspoon salt
4 whole eggs or 8 egg whites

Salt and pepper tomato slices to taste. In a large nonstick skillet, heat 2 tablespoons olive oil over medium heat. Add the tomato slices, sauté until hot, and remove to 4 plates.

Wipe the pan dry and add a few drops more olive oil. Return pan to heat and add the pine nuts. Gently toss the nuts until golden brown and set aside. Add the spinach and chicory or dandelion leaves, tossing gently. Add the nutmeg, tarragon, and chives and cook 2 minutes more. Add salt and pepper to taste. Set aside.

Following directions on page 102, poach the eggs.

While the eggs are cooking, divide the greens into 4 servings, swirl with a fork to create nests, and set each serving on a tomato slice. With fingertips, make a hollow in the greens.

When the eggs are done, place each one in a greens nest. Sprinkle the pine nuts over the greens and serve at once.

Variation

If you can't find chicory or dandelion leaves, you can substitute arugula or other greens, or simply increase the spinach to 4 cups.

Eggs Benedict

No breakfast recipe book would be complete without a recipe for this incredibly rich treat. My advice is to limit the amount of Hollandaise sauce you use. This recipe makes about 3/4 cup Hollandaise sauce.

MAKES 4 SERVINGS.

About 4 tablespoons Hollandaise Sauce
 (see opposite) or commercial Hollandaise
 sauce (see Note below)
4 eggs
4 English muffin halves
4 thin slices reduced-fat cooked ham

Hollandaise Sauce
3 egg yolks
1/4 cup water
2 tablespoons fresh lemon juice
8 tablespoons cold butter, cut into 8 pieces
Dash each of salt, paprika, and
 ground red pepper

Prepare Hollandaise Sauce: Beat egg yolks, water, and lemon juice and cook over very low heat, stirring constantly, until the mixture bubbles at the edges. Stir in butter, 1 piece at a time, until the butter melts and the mixture thickens very gently over very low heat.

Poach 4 eggs according to the directions on page 102. Toast English muffin halves.

Spray a medium nonstick frying pan with nonstick cooking spray and quickly heat the ham over high heat, a few seconds per side.

Put 1 ham slice on each muffin half. Place poached eggs on top of ham slices and spoon on Hollandaise sauce.

Variations

You may use a thin slice of tomato instead of the ham, or a thick slice of grilled tomato instead of the muffin.

Note

Commercial Hollandaise sauce works well in this recipe. Warm sauce very gently over very low heat before serving.

Mushroom and Chèvre Omelette

There must be fifty ways to make an omelette, or more. Adding ingredients to an omelette is a bit trickier than with scrambled eggs because you have to be careful about the texture and weight of the ingredients. Try these recipes and then create your own.

MAKES 1 OR 2 SERVINGS.

2 eggs
1 teaspoon milk
Salt and pepper to taste

2 mushrooms, thinly sliced
1 ounce chèvre (goat cheese)
1 tablespoon chopped fresh chives

Beat together eggs, milk, salt, and pepper in a small bowl and cook omelette as described on pages 102–103.

Scatter mushrooms on one side of the omelette and then crumble the chèvre over mushrooms. Continue cooking according to directions. To serve, sprinkle chives over finished omelette.

Variations

Caviar Omelette

Fill with 2 teaspoons caviar and 1 teaspoon sour cream.

Spinach Omelette

Sauté 2 thin onion slices over medium-low heat until tender. Add 4 or 5 spinach leaves and a dash of nutmeg and cook a few minutes until the spinach wilts; drain and set aside. Instead of milk, stir 1 tablespoon ricotta cheese into egg mixture and make omelette according to directions on pages 102–103, using spinach mixture as filling.

Lox Omelette

Use 2 tablespoons minced smoked salmon and 1 teaspoon cream cheese as a filling. Serve with—what else?—a toasted bagel.

Artichoke-Pepper Omelette

Drain an artichoke heart and chop coarsely. Toss 2 tablespoons minced red bell pepper with artichoke hearts, a pinch of onion powder, and salt and pepper to taste. (I prefer the crunch of the uncooked pepper in this filling but you may elect to sauté and drain the pepper ahead of time.) Prepare omelette as described on pages 102–103, using artichoke-pepper mixture as a filling. Sprinkle a little chopped green onion over the finished omelette before serving.

Apple-Cheddar Omelette

Take a tip from Blanche's B & B in Franconia, New Hampshire, and stir a dash of dried dill into your eggs. For the filling, use 1/4 apple, finely chopped, and 2 tablespoons grated sharp Cheddar cheese.

Ratatouille Omelette

Make good use of your leftover ratatouille and use it as a filling in your next omelette.

Perfect Baked Eggs

Here's how my mom taught me to make baked eggs. This method cannot be improved upon.

MAKES 4 BAKED EGGS.

2 teaspoons margarine, butter, or oil
1/2 clove garlic, minced
1/2 medium onion, finely chopped

4 eggs
4 tablespoons grated hard cheese:
    Cheddar, Swiss, etc.

Preheat the oven to 425F (220C). Add margarine, butter, or oil to individual nonstick ramekins or a larger nonstick baking dish.

Heat dishes in oven about 5 minutes or until the fat is hot and sizzling. Remove dishes from oven and add the garlic and onion. Carefully break eggs into dishes and sprinkle with cheese.

Return dishes to the oven, reduce heat to 350F (175C), and cook 5 to 10 minutes or until the whites are set and yolks are still soft or about 15 minutes or until yolks are hard.

Variations

To bake an egg in a toast cup, press a slice of bread gently with a rolling pin and then press it into a 6-ounce ramekin or muffin cup that has been sprayed with nonstick cooking spray. Brush with melted butter and/or sprinkle with garlic powder or cinnamon and sugar, if desired. Bake at 400F (205C) about 5 minutes until the toast is lightly browned, then add the egg and proceed as directed on page 102.

To bake an egg in a tomato cup, remove the top quarter of the tomato and scoop out the seeds and pulp. Place the tomato in a ramekin or muffin cup that has been sprayed with nonstick cooking spray. Break in an egg. Sprinkle on some chèvre or other cheese and minced fresh herbs. Proceed as directed on page 102.

To bake an egg in a potato, cut a baked potato in half lengthwise. Scoop out most of the meat of the potato, mash with 1 tablespoon milk, and return most of the mashed potato to the shell. Make a well in the center of each mashed potato half, break in an egg, and bake according to directions on page 102.

To bake an egg in stuffing, use your favorite leftover stuffing, such as bread, rice, or sausage stuffing. (Needless to say, if the stuffing was originally part of a meat or poultry dish, it should have been properly prepared and removed from the meat or poultry immediately after cooking and then refrigerated.) Spray a ramekin or muffin cup with nonstick cooking spray. Spoon in the stuffing and add a few drops of milk or broth if it has dried out. Make a well in the stuffing and crack in an egg. Lay strips of meat (such as turkey) across the top and bake at 375F (190C) about 20 minutes until egg is set and stuffing is cooked through.

High Meadows Classic Egg Cups

Here's a delightful one-dish meal from the High Meadows Vineyard and Mountain Sunset in Albemarle County, Virginia. Serve with the inn's apple-strudel muffins (page 42) for a foolproof breakfast.

MAKES 4 EGG CUPS.

4 slices cooked meat: turkey, Canadian
   bacon, etc.
4 eggs

4 tablespoons grated Gruyère cheese
4 thin slices tomato
Fresh parsley or basil

Preheat oven to 350F (175C). Spray 4 (6-ounce) ramekins or muffin cups with nonstick cooking spray. Gently press 1 slice of meat into each cup to form a container. Break an egg into each meat container and top with cheese, tomato, and parsley or basil.

Bake 20 to 30 minutes or until eggs are set. Use a knife to gently lift the meat and egg out of the ramekin or muffin cup onto a plate. (The meat will flatten out while the egg will retain its shape.)

Traditional Huevos Rancheros

This traditional Tex-Mex dish deserves a place at every table.

MAKES 6 SERVINGS.

6 corn tortillas
1 1/2 cloves garlic, minced
1 medium yellow onion, chopped
1 red bell pepper, chopped
1 to 2 green chiles, finely minced
   (see Note below)

2 tablespoons minced fresh cilantro
3 to 4 ripe tomatoes, coarsely chopped
6 eggs
1/3 cup plain yogurt or sour cream
1/3 cup shredded Monterey Jack cheese

Preheat the oven to 350F (175C). Spray a nonstick 13 × 9-inch pan with nonstick cooking spray.

Spray a large nonstick frying pan with nonstick cooking spray and place over medium-high heat. Quickly fry each tortilla, a few seconds per side, until the tortilla softens slightly. Transfer tortillas to prepared pan, allowing them to overlap and to curl up the sides of the pan.

Spray the frying pan again and place over medium-low heat. Sauté garlic and onion about 5 minutes or until onion softens. Stir in bell pepper, chiles, and cilantro and sauté another 2 minutes. Add the tomatoes and continue cooking 5 to 10 minutes or until the mixture is a soft and chunky salsa. Spread this mixture evenly over the tortillas.

With the back of a spoon, make 6 depressions in the salsa. Break an egg into each depression. Top each egg with a spoonful of yogurt or sour cream and then sprinkle with cheese.

Bake, uncovered, 15 to 20 minutes or until eggs are set.

Note

For a spicier salsa, include chile seeds. For milder salsa, remove the chile seeds before mincing.

Easy Huevos Rancheros

I was in the midst of trying out recipes for huevos rancheros (comparing proportions of tomatoes to chiles and so on), when the phone rang and my mother gave me this easy version.

MAKES 4 HUEVOS RANCHEROS.

1/2 cup commercial salsa

4 eggs

4 teaspoons plain yogurt or sour cream

4 tablespoons grated hard cheese:
    Monterey Jack, Cheddar, etc.

Preheat the oven to 350F (175C). Lightly grease 4 (6-ounce) ramekins.

Put the ramekins in the oven for a few minutes until they're hot. Remove them and divide the salsa among the dishes. Break an egg into the center of the salsa in each dish. To each egg, add 1 teaspoon of yogurt or sour cream and sprinkle with 1 tablespoon of cheese. Cover with foil.

Bake about 15 minutes or until eggs are set. Serve in the ramekins.

Variation

Quickly heat 4 tortillas, one at a time, in a lightly oiled frying pan about 1 minute per side and then press each tortilla into a ramekin or muffin cup to form a container. Add the other ingredients and bake as described in recipe.

Cappuccino Eggs

Under the heading "What will they think of next?" comes this scrambled egg recipe I picked up at my local coffee shop. You'll need a cappuccino maker.

MAKES 1 SERVING.

2 eggs

2 teaspoons milk

In a cup, beat together the egg and the milk. Put the nozzle of the milk steamer into the egg mixture and steam a few minutes until the mixture is cooked through and fluffy.

Florentine Frittata

With all the flavors and aromas of its motherland, this frittata can't be beat.

MAKES 2 HEARTY OR 3 OR 4 SMALLER SERVINGS.

4 eggs
1/4 cup ricotta cheese
2 tablespoons olive oil
1/4 teaspoon ground nutmeg
Salt and black pepper to taste
1/4 cup sliced mushrooms
1 clove garlic, minced

2 green onions, chopped
1 teaspoon mixed dried herbs
2 cups rinsed, dried, and coarsely chopped
    fresh spinach
1/2 red bell pepper, cut into strips
2 tablespoons grated Cheddar cheese
1/4 cup grated mozzarella cheese

Preheat broiler. In a small bowl, mix the eggs, ricotta, 1 teaspoon of the oil, nutmeg, salt, and black pepper.

Heat the remaining oil in an 8-inch cast-iron pan (or other stovetop-to-oven pan) and sauté mushrooms, garlic, and green onions over medium heat 2 minutes. Add herbs, spinach, and bell pepper and cook another 2 minutes or until spinach is reduced but not completely wilted.

Remove the pan from the heat and sprinkle with the Cheddar cheese. Spread vegetables evenly over the bottom of the pan and pour on the egg-ricotta mixture. Return to the heat 2 minutes, then sprinkle with the mozzarella cheese.

Broil 2 minutes or until eggs are set and cheese is bubbly. Slide the frittata onto a serving dish, cut into wedges and serve at once.

1024 Washington Italian Frittata

Here's a tasty frittata with zingy flavor, served at 1024 Washington, a bed and breakfast in Bath, Maine.

MAKES 2 HEARTY OR 3 OR 4 SMALLER SERVINGS.

2 teaspoons olive oil

2 tablespoons peeled and cubed potato

1 sweet Italian sausage

1 tablespoon chopped yellow onion

1 tablespoon chopped red bell pepper

1/2 clove garlic, minced

4 eggs

2 teaspoons milk

1/8 teaspoon dried oregano

1 tablespoon shredded mozzarella cheese

4 thin slices tomato

1 tablespoon grated Cheddar cheese

1 tablespoon minced Italian parsley

Preheat broiler. Heat olive oil in an 8-inch cast-iron (or other stovetop-to-oven) pan over medium-high heat. Add potato and sauté 5 to 10 minutes or until it begins to soften.

Remove casing from sausage and crumble into pan with potato. Cook, stirring occasionally, another 5 minutes or until the sausage has browned. Add the onion, bell pepper, and garlic and continue cooking until the onion is translucent and the potato fully softened, 5 to 10 minutes.

Put eggs, milk, and oregano in the blender and process until smooth. Pour egg mixture and mozzarella over the potato mixture. Reduce the heat and cook, stirring lightly, until the eggs are soft and fluffy. Remove from heat.

Space 4 tomato slices evenly around the pan and sprinkle the Cheddar cheese on the eggs. Cook under the broiler for barely a minute or until cheese melts.

To serve, top with parsley. Cut into wedges, with a tomato in each wedge.

Irish Frittata

Here's an elegant way to serve eggs and spuds!

MAKES 2 HEARTY OR 3 OR 4 SMALLER SERVINGS.

1 Russet potato, peeled and cubed
2 teaspoons olive oil
1/2 yellow onion, finely chopped
4 eggs

1/4 teaspoon dried rosemary or
   1 teaspoon fresh minced rosemary
2 tablespoons cream cheese
1/4 cup shredded Cheddar cheese

Preheat broiler. Place the potato in a small saucepan and cover with water. Bring to a boil and cook about 10 minutes until potato is tender but still firm. Drain well on paper towels.

Heat oil in a 10-inch cast-iron (or other stovetop-to-oven) pan over medium-low heat and sauté the onion until translucent, about 10 minutes. Add the potato and continue cooking until the potato is heated through.

Beat the eggs with the rosemary and pour them into the pan. Dot with pieces of cream cheese, spacing them evenly around the pan. Cook another 5 minutes on top of the stove.

Sprinkle with the Cheddar cheese and broil about 5 minutes or until the cheese is hot and bubbly. Cut into wedges.

Variation

For an attractive presentation, scatter sprigs of fresh rosemary around the plate.

Frittata Primavera

This frittata uses bread crumbs for added body.

MAKES 2 HEARTY OR 3 OR 4 SMALLER SERVINGS.

4 eggs

2 tablespoons seasoned bread crumbs

Salt and pepper to taste

1 tablespoon mixed, minced fresh herbs:
   chives, basil, oregano

1/4 cup ricotta cheese

2 teaspoons olive oil

1/4 head broccoli or cauliflower,
   cut into small flowerets

1 zucchini, sliced

1/2 red bell pepper, diced

1 carrot, grated

1 green onion, thinly sliced

2 tablespoons frozen green peas,
   thawed and drained

2 tablespoons grated mozzarella cheese

Preheat broiler. In a medium bowl, beat the eggs and stir in the bread crumbs, salt, pepper, herbs, and ricotta cheese.

In a 10-inch cast-iron (or other stovetop-to-oven) pan, heat the olive oil over medium-high heat. Add the broccoli or cauliflower and stir-fry about 2 minutes. Add zucchini and stir-fry about 2 minutes. Add bell pepper and stir-fry about 2 minutes. Add carrot, green onion and peas and stir-fry about 2 minutes.

Pour on the egg mixture. Cook another 5 to 10 minutes on top of the stove or until the eggs have just set.

Sprinkle with mozzarella cheese and broil about 2 minutes or until the cheese is bubbly. Cut into wedges.

Side Dishes

What do you serve with your single fried egg? A tasty side dish, of course. Something familiar but revitalized, like Oven-Baked Hash Browns (page 121), for instance, or maybe something excitingly new like Seafood Hash (page 125).

Of course, you can easily enjoy these dishes without eggs. I hope that you'll use this book to create a mix-and-match menu of dishes that add up to a wholesome meal. Try Seafood Hash (page 125) with Gingered Melon (page 21) and a slice of Mrs. Flanagan's Irish Soda Bread (page 53), for instance. Or serve grilled vegetables (page 124) with Southern Spoon Bread (page 51) and a blender drink (pages 34–38).

Mushroom and Spinach Sauté

There are enough vitamins and minerals in this dish to shoot you out the door in the morning. And the good news is this dish has practically no calories. As you know if you've cooked fresh spinach before, the huge bag of spinach you bring home from the market will cook down to a handful of cooked greens, so don't be stingy!

MAKES 4 TO 6 SERVINGS.

1 teaspoon olive oil
1 clove garlic, crushed
1/2 small Bermuda onion, thinly sliced
1/2 pound mixed mushrooms,
  wiped clean and sliced

4 cups fresh spinach, rinsed and dried
1/4 teaspoon ground pepper
1/4 teaspoon ground nutmeg

Heat the oil in a large nonstick saucepan over medium-low heat and sauté the garlic and onion until onion is translucent, 5 to 10 minutes. Add the mushrooms and sauté until tender but not soft, about 5 minutes.

Add the spinach, pepper, and nutmeg and increase heat to high to quickly reduce moisture and wilt the spinach. (The residual moisture in the mushrooms and the spinach should make it possible to avoid adding extra oil.) Cook until spinach is wilted. Serve at once.

Variations

Instead of mushrooms, add 1/2 cup currants and 1/2 cup toasted almonds or 1/4 cup pine nuts to the sautéed spinach and cook for another 2 minutes before serving.

Oven-Baked Hash Browns

Here's a low-fat alternative to this breakfast favorite.

MAKES 4 TO 6 SERVINGS.

2 medium red potatoes, peeled and cubed
1 small red onion
2 teaspoons olive oil

1 pinch of dried rosemary
Salt and pepper to taste

Cook the potatoes in boiling water about 15 minutes or until softened but not mushy. Drain and let cool. (You can do this the night before and refrigerate the potatoes.)

Preheat the oven to 400F (205C). Spray a nonstick baking sheet with nonstick cooking spray.

Peel and dice the red onion and toss lightly with the potatoes, olive oil, rosemary, salt and pepper. Spoon potato mixture into prepared baking dish. Bake about 30 minutes or until browned, stirring twice during cooking.

Variation

Dice a slice of lean ham and toss with the potatoes and onion.

Smoked-Salmon Quesadilla

From the Molly Stark Inn in Bennington, Vermont, comes this distinctly non–New England dish. Half a quesadilla makes a superb side dish; a whole quesadilla is a meal in itself.

MAKES 2 SIDE-DISH SERVINGS OR 1 MAIN COURSE.

3/4 cup sour cream
1 tablespoon chopped fresh dill
1 (10-inch) flour tortilla
2 ounces Boursin cheese
1 plum tomato, chopped

1 teaspoon chopped fresh dill
2 ounces smoked salmon
1/2 teaspoon capers (optional)
1 red onion, cut in half and sliced crosswise

Prepare a topping by mixing the sour cream with the dill; set aside.

Bring the tortilla to room temperature. Spread the cheese on half the tortilla. Top with chopped tomato, dill, salmon slices, and capers, if using. Fold the tortilla in half and press lightly on edges.

Spray a medium nonstick saucepan with nonstick cooking spray. Sauté tortilla over medium heat until golden brown, about 5 minutes. Turn over and brown the other side.

Cut the quesadilla in half. Serve warm with sour cream mixture and slices of onion.

Sweet Potato Puree

A dollop of these fragrant potatoes goes beautifully with egg dishes. You can even use it as a spread on bagels and other breads.

MAKES 4 SERVINGS.

2 sweet potatoes, peeled and cubed
1/4 cup buttermilk

2 teaspoons butter or margarine

Cook the sweet potatoes in boiling water about 25 minutes or until tender. Drain the sweet potatoes.

Put the drained sweet potatoes and remaining ingredients in a blender and puree until smooth.

Serve at once or refrigerate overnight and reheat in a small ovenproof nonstick pan at 350F (175C) 20 minutes or until heated through.

Mixed Grill

This staple of English country house breakfasts is a low-fat way to beef up your breakfast.
(Vegetarian houseguests live on it!)

MAKES 4 SERVINGS.

2 red onions, cut into wedges
1/2 pound mushrooms, wiped clean
2 plum tomatoes, cut in half lengthwise

1 tablespoon olive oil
Salt and pepper to taste

Preheat broiler. On a broiler pan rack set over pan to catch juices, arrange vegetables, then drizzle with the oil and season with salt and pepper.

Broil 5 to 10 minutes, turning once, until vegetables are soft, browned, or even slightly blackened, to your taste.

Variation

Dip the vegetables in egg or milk and then coat them with bread crumbs or a mixture of cornmeal and flour, arrange on the rack, and broil about 10 minutes or until browned.

Seafood Hash

You'll love this alternative to corned beef hash.

MAKES 6 SERVINGS.

1 1/2 teaspoons olive oil
1/2 red onion, diced
1 clove garlic (optional), minced
2 medium Russet potatoes, peeled and
    diced
1/4 red bell pepper, diced
1 cup cooked fresh or canned seafood:
    salmon, crab, tuna, bass, etc.

1 medium tomato, diced
2 teaspoons tomato paste
2 teaspoons fresh lemon juice
1/2 teaspoon dried thyme
1 1/2 teaspoons sugar (optional)

Heat oil in a large nonstick pot over medium heat and sauté the onion and garlic, if using, about 5 minutes or until onion starts to soften.

Parboil potatoes 5 minutes and then drain well. Add the drained potato to the pot and continue sautéing until potatoes are lightly browned and softened. Add the bell pepper, seafood, tomato, tomato paste, lemon juice, thyme, and sugar, if using. Cook another 5 to 10 minutes or until all the ingredients are cooked through.

Variation

Substitute 1 sweet potato for 1 Russet potato.

Kids' Favorites

In my imaginary life, I rise a good hour before the rest of my family, pull on a lace dressing gown, and head for the kitchen, where I whip up a beautiful three-course meal of fresh fruit salad, home-baked muffins, and made-to-order waffles. My husband and children arrive, fully dressed, in the dining room, where we all talk meaningfully over my delicious meal. Forty-five minutes later, I wave good-bye to them from the doorstep, scoop up the newspaper, pour myself a cup of coffee, and spend the next half-hour relaxing in bed.

In my real life, mornings often begin when my younger child leaps from the foot of my bed onto my stomach. I cast a bleary eye at the alarm clock and realize that I've overslept. I stagger out of the bedroom into the hall, where I meet my older child, who tells me she's run out of clean T-shirts. By the time we're all dressed and washed, I may have as little as half an hour to feed my family before we all scramble out the door.

That's why, every night before I go to bed, I set the table for breakfast. I can already hear you groaning when you read this, but all I can say is: try it. It's much easier to find fifteen minutes to set the table, load the coffee maker, lay out the pans and provisions you'll need in the kitchen, and so on, in the evening than it is to find that same fifteen minutes the next morning.

A Good Start

If breakfast is important for adults, it's vital for kids. A number of studies have linked eating breakfast to better performance at school. In one study conducted in Jamaica, for instance, undernourished children (whose weight for age was well under the average) were given school breakfasts. When they were tested for verbal fluency, their performance improved significantly. And there is evidence that even generally well-nourished children are better able to concentrate in school when they've eaten a wholesome breakfast.

There are other benefits to breakfast, too. Dr. William Cochran, pediatric gastroenterologist and nutritionist at the Geisinger Clinic in Danville, Pennsylvania, says, "Eating a proper breakfast is important from an overall nutritional standpoint. It encourages good eating habits and eating schedules. A child who is accustomed to starting the day with a good breakfast at home is less likely to grab a candy bar later in the day. The child will have a healthier eating pattern."

A Healthy Breakfast

The good news is you don't need to go through hoops (or get up half an hour earlier) to provide a healthy breakfast for your child. A child's morning dietary needs are not much different from an adult's. Look for foods that are low in fat and sugar content, provide fiber, and meet a good percentage of the Recommended Daily Allowances. The American Academy of Pediatrics recommends that the calories in your child's breakfast be composed of 55 percent carbohydrates, no more than 30 percent fat, and 15 percent protein. That means that a humble meal like cereal with milk and a glass of juice is actually a nutritious start to your child's day.

The recipes that follow are fast and simple. They're also fun to make with kids, so enlist some little helpers in your kitchen.

Breakfast Fun

Here are some quick and easy tips that will overcome even the most reluctant kid's resistance to breakfast.

Fruit Fondue   Prepare bite-sized pieces of fruit: halved strawberries, melon balls, grapes, chunks of apple, pineapple, pear, etc. Serve them with a bowl of your child's favorite yogurt. Let her dip the fruit into the yogurt.

Happy-Face Pancakes   When you're making pancakes, have ready an assortment of cut fruit. Using small dollops of jelly as an adhesive, create faces on your cooked pancake by adding, for instance, blueberry eyes, a line of raspberries for a mouth, and a banana-wedge nose. Mandarin orange sections might form curly hair.

Fruit Cones   Mix fresh berries or other fruit into yogurt and spoon the mixture into ice cream cones for a tempting treat.

Crazy Flakes   If your child is hooked on sweetened cereals, try mixing sweetened flakes with unsweetened, to limit the sugar content.

Banana Boat   Spoon some blueberry yogurt onto a plate to make a lake. Peel the banana and place it, rounded side down, in the yogurt. Using yogurt or jam as an adhesive, place O-shaped cereals along the sides of the boat to make portholes. Attach strawberry-wedge "sails" with blunt toothpicks.

Breakwich   Toast frozen waffles, spread with peanut butter, and layer on sliced banana for an open-face sandwich. Or pop two slices of bread in the toaster and puree cottage cheese and strawberries in the blender. Spread the strawberry-cheese mixture on the toast and close to make sandwiches.

Mexfast   Tortillas are a fun change of pace for breakfast. To avoid cooking in fat, wrap a tortilla in foil and bake it for 10 minutes in a preheated 250F (120C) oven. Scramble an egg and roll it up in the warmed tortilla. Or spread peanut butter and jelly or cream cheese and grated carrot on the tortilla and roll it up like a jelly roll.

French Toast Cut-outs   Before dipping your bread in egg and milk, get out your cookie cutters and cut the bread into fun shapes.

Better Breads   Perk up breakfast with a different kind of bread: choose whole-wheat English muffins or bagels, try rice cakes spread with low-fat cheese, or fill a pita pocket with your child's favorite spread.

Breakfast Parfait   If your child is old enough to be trusted with a glass, layer yogurt, fresh fruit, and breakfast cereal in a parfait glass. (Or use a clear plastic container.) Serve on a linen placemat with a lovely flower.

Dr. Cochran's Jammy Bran Muffins

Dr. Cochran hands out this recipe to his patients' moms, hoping that they'll try this high-fiber, low-fat breakfast treat. One of the great things about this recipe is that you can make the batter up to three days in advance, which means that in the morning, all you have to do is to fill the required number of muffin cups with batter and jam and pop them in the oven while the family gets dressed and ready for breakfast. Or bake ahead of time (it's a very kid-friendly recipe) and warm up in the oven or microwave.

MAKES 12 LARGE MUFFINS.

1 1/2 cups all-purpose flour
3/4 cup sugar
1 teaspoon baking powder
1/4 teaspoon baking soda
1/4 teaspoon salt
1 cup buttermilk

1/4 cup vegetable oil
1 egg
4 cups bran flakes
1/4 cup fruit-sweetened jam or jelly
   (your child's favorite kind)

Preheat the oven to 350F (175C). Spray 12 nonstick muffin cups with nonstick cooking spray.

Combine the flour, sugar, baking powder, baking soda, and salt in a large bowl.

In a medium bowl, combine buttermilk, oil, and egg. Add liquid ingredients to dry ingredients and mix just enough to blend. Fold in the bran flakes.

Fill each muffin cup half full with batter. Spoon 1 teaspoon of jam or jelly into the center of the batter in each muffin cup. Cover with remaining batter.

Bake 20 to 25 minutes or until a wooden pick comes out clean. (Don't overbake.) Turn out muffins onto a wire rack to cool.

Variations

Reduce the sugar in this recipe as much as you wish. Use raisin bran instead of bran flakes and (for older children) stir in some chopped nuts.

Breakfast Pizza

Breakfast pizza? As a matter of fact, many kids like a slice of last night's pizza warmed up for breakfast, and it's not a bad choice, nutritionally speaking. This is an adaptation most people (kids and adults) will find more appealing in the morning.

MAKES 4 PIZZAS.

1 package pizza mix (for making 1 pizza crust)
8 ounces small curd cottage cheese
1/2 teaspoon pure vanilla extract
1/2 teaspoon ground cinnamon

2 tablespoons sugar (optional)
1 cup sliced fruit: strawberries, peaches, oranges, blueberries, apple, banana, etc.
4 tablespoons fruit-sweetened peach or apricot jelly

Preheat oven to 425F (220C). Spray a nonstick baking sheet with nonstick cooking spray.

Following package directions, prepare pizza dough and form 4 small pizzas, each about 5 inches in diameter. Turn up the edges to form a pizza crust.

Mix together the cottage cheese, vanilla, cinnamon, and sugar, if using. Spread this mixture over the crust and artfully arrange the fruit on top of the cheese mixture.

In a small saucepan, heat the jelly over low heat until slightly melted. Spread it over the fruit. (The jelly will seal and glaze the fruit.)

Bake 15 to 20 minutes or until the pizza crust is golden brown.

Variation

If you don't have time to make the pizza dough, replace it with an English muffin or refrigerator biscuit dough.

Egg in the Basket

Here's an old favorite that still tastes great. (Your family may know it as Toad in the Hole, Bull's Eye, or Knothole Eggs.)

MAKES 1 SERVING.

1 slice bread   1 egg

Heat a nonstick pan over high heat, then turn down the heat to medium. Spray with non-stick cooking spray.

    Cut a circle out of the center of a slice of bread. Put the bread in the hot pan and then break the egg into the hole. When toast is brown on the bottom, flip it (the egg should flip inside the toast). When both sides are cooked, transfer to a plate and serve. (If your child doesn't like whole yolks, mix up the egg in a cup before pouring into the hole.)

Peachy-Keen Fruit Drink

Kids love "milkshakes" made from combinations of fruit, milk, and yogurt. Make sure yogurt and milk are icy cold when you begin. This is just one version; experiment with your own.

MAKES 1 DRINK, ABOUT 8 OUNCES.

1 peach, peeled and cut into chunks   1/3 cup low-fat milk
1/3 cup peach or vanilla yogurt   2 ice cubes

Combine peach, yogurt, milk, and ice cubes in a blender and process at high speed until the ice is dispersed through the drink. Serve at once.

Variation

For extra protein, add 1 tablespoon of wheat germ or peanut butter.

Eggs to Go

For the teenager who spends all morning deciding which pair of jeans to wear to school and then doesn't have time for breakfast, here's a meal that can be eaten at the bus stop.

MAKES 1 SERVING.

1 English muffin   2 eggs
1 thick slice cooked turkey or ham

Slice the English muffin in half and toast it in the toaster.

In a medium nonstick pan over medium heat, sauté the slice of turkey or ham. Transfer to one side of the toasted English muffin.

In the same pan, scramble eggs according to directions on pages 101–102, using nonstick cooking spray if needed.

Pile the egg on top of the turkey or ham, close the muffin, wrap in foil, and hand the sandwich to the teenager as he or she heads out the door.

Variations

If the teenager is a lacto-ovo vegetarian, eliminate meat and stir grated cheese into the egg. If the teenager is a vegan, eliminate the meat and eggs and make scrambled tofu.

Oatmeal-Jam Bars

A great on-the-go treat for busy teenagers, these will be equally popular with younger kids.

MAKES ABOUT 8 BARS.

1 1/4 cups all-purpose flour
1/2 teaspoon baking soda
1/4 teaspoon salt
3/4 cup rolled oats
2 (3-ounce) packages cream cheese,
    softened

1/4 cup butter or margarine, softened
1/4 cup packed brown sugar
1/2 cup fruit-sweetened jam
1/4 cup finely chopped nuts (optional)

Preheat oven to 350F (175C). Spray an 8-inch-square nonstick baking dish with nonstick cooking spray.

In a large bowl, combine flour, baking soda, and salt. Stir in rolled oats.

In a medium bowl, cream together cream cheese and butter or margarine with the back of a fork. Stir in the brown sugar and mix until well blended.

Add the cream cheese mixture to the dry ingredients and combine.

Spread 2/3 of the mixture in the prepared pan. Bake 15 minutes. Remove from oven and spread jam over cooked oat layer. Stir nuts, if using, into remaining oatmeal mixture and sprinkle this mixture on top of the jam.

Bake another 20 minutes, until top of oatmeal mixture is lightly browned. Cool, then cut into bars and serve.

Fruit Salad with Banana Dressing

The sweet flavor of banana is a true kid-pleaser.

MAKES ABOUT 1 1/4 CUPS.

1/4 ripe banana
2 tablespoons plain, banana, or
    vanilla yogurt

1 tablespoon orange juice
1 cup of your child's favorite fruit mixture

Combine banana, yogurt, and orange juice in a blender and process until smooth. Toss with the fruit.

Governor's Inn Grahamcakes

From the Governor's Inn in Ludlow, Vermont, here's an irresistible treat for anyone who loves graham crackers.

MAKES 10 TO 12 PANCAKES.

3/4 cup all-purpose flour
3/4 cup graham cracker crumbs
1 tablespoon baking powder
1/4 teaspoon salt

1 cup milk
2 tablespoons butter or margarine, melted
1 egg

Combine flour, cracker crumbs, baking powder, and salt in a large bowl.

In a small bowl, mix milk, butter or margarine, and egg. Add liquid ingredients to dry ingredients and mix well to form a thick batter.

Cook pancakes on a hot griddle over medium-high heat, following the instructions on page 66.

Variations

Your child may prefer thinner pancakes; if so, add another 1/2 cup milk. Also, if your child is old enough to eat nuts, mix in 1/2 cup chopped pecans after combining dry and liquid ingredients.

Hot Drinks

In 1669 Soleiman Aga, the Turkish ambassador to Louis XIV, introduced coffee to the Western world. Elegantly attired and turbaned, sporting smudges of kohl around his eyes, he poured his exotic brew into tiny saucers made of silver and gold, and served it to the ladies and gentlemen of Louis's court. He created a passion that hasn't abated in over three hundred years.

For most of us, breakfast isn't complete without a steaming mug of something hot and caffeinated—coffee, tea, or at the very least hot chocolate. One of the great indignities of life in America today is the dictum that caffeine is unhealthy. If your doctor will allow you only one cup of coffee a day, do have it with your morning meal.

Happily, the new range of decaffeinated coffees and herbal teas offer plenty of variety and choice to the former caffeine addict who's been cast adrift in a nutritionally correct sea. Try them in the recipes that follow or embrace an altogether different hot drink—Hot Lemonade (page 149) or steaming Cranberry Punch (page 148), for example.

Coffee

How do you make the perfect cup of coffee? Some aspects of coffee making are a matter of taste; others are irrefutable rules. Keep these points in mind:

Equipment   Whether you use a perculator or an espresso maker or countertop automatic coffee maker is up to you. Make sure, though, that the equipment you use gets the water really hot; otherwise your coffee will be disappointing. Just below boiling is the proper temperature for water that is passing through coffee grounds. Make sure to keep your equipment scrupulously clean: a cleaning solution of one part baking soda to five parts water will give you spotless equipment.

Water   The flavor of the water you use to make coffee will affect the taste of the coffee. If you like the taste of your tap water, by all means use it, but be sure that it is cold when you begin the coffee-making process. If your tap water has an unappealing, chemical flavor, consider using bottled water instead.

Freshness   The best coffee comes from beans that are ground on the spot, just before preparing the coffee. (And the aroma of freshly ground coffee is a heavenly smell first thing in the morning.) Use the proper grind (fine, coarse, etc.) for your coffee maker. Too fine will cause bitterness, but too coarse will result in weak coffee. Don't buy ten bags of coffee at a time; try to buy small amounts frequently for maximum freshness. Store your beans, or ground coffee if you don't grind your own, in a tightly sealed container in a cool, dark place. You can freeze coffee beans but it's not a good idea to take them in and out of the freezer every time you make a cup of coffee, since this causes condensation. A pot of brewed coffee will remain tasty for up to half an hour. If you can't be bothered making a fresh pot every half hour, pour brewed coffee into a Thermos®.

The Beans   Although freshness is probably the most important part of a good cup of coffee, the choice of beans is also vital. Because there is considerable variation in the harvesting process—the ripeness of the bean when picked, the amount of time it is allowed to ferment and dry in the sun, and so on—the more expensive "specialty" coffee lines may actually offer more than just a fancy label. Once harvested, coffee is roasted. Americans tend to favor a light roast, which is milder but arguably more flavorful, whereas Europeans prefer a dark roast, which makes good strong espresso coffee drinks. When you select beans you must know what kind of roast you prefer and also which country's coffee beans you prefer.

The names of countries where coffee is grown—Brazil, Colombia, Yemen, Costa Rica, Jamaica, and Kenya, to name only a few—are exotic and flavorful in themselves, and you will probably find that you prefer the coffees grown in certain countries. Coffee experts—much like wine tasters—have their own specialized terminology to describe the flavors of different beans: they use terms like *winey, smoky, mild-bodied,* and *mellow.* Unless you're versed in the lingo, the best way to choose coffee is to smell and ideally taste it. Many companies offer blends that you may find appealing. In addition, the roaster may have added a flavor, like vanilla or butterscotch, to the beans.

All About Decaf Even among coffee beans that are not decaffeinated, caffeine content varies. The darker the roast, for instance, the less caffeine in the bean. Different coffee plants produce different degrees of caffeination, too: from 170 milligrams in a 6-ounce cup of Costa Rican coffee to 327 milligrams in the same amount of Robusta Uganda! To decaffeinate coffee, either water or a chemical solvent is passed through coffee beans to wash away the caffeine. The Swiss water process is more expensive but aficionados prefer it both for the flavor of the beans produced and for the presumed health benefits of a natural decaffeination method.

Tea

"The agony of the leaves" is the tea connoisseur's evocative description of what happens when boiling water comes into contact with loose tea leaves: the leaves unfold and release their pungent flavor into the water. From the Japanese tea ceremony to English afternoon tea, *Camellia sinensis*—the evergreen cousin to the flowering camellia bush—inspires both ritual and a sense of mystery in its devotees.

Good health may be inspired by tea-drinking, too. A recent study found that black and green tea contain flavonoids, which help reduce the risk of heart attack.

Choosing Tea

The *flush,* a tea connoisseur's term, describes the virginal new growth which provides the most flavorful teas and which is at its best in spring. The finest teas are made from the flush.

Once harvested, tea leaves are treated in one of three ways: green tea is made from unfermented tea leaves that have been steamed and gently rolled and heated; the finest grade is Gunpowder. Black tea, the kind most of us are used to, is fermented and then dried and sorted by size and color. Finally, oolong teas fall somewhere between green and black; they are slightly fermented.

Once this first treatment is completed, the tea harvester may add in a scent (such as jasmine), a flavor (such as orange), and/or a spice (such as cinnamon). Finally, a variety of tea leaves will probably be combined into a blend. Earl Grey and Irish Breakfast teas are examples of popular blends.

Herbal teas, known in Europe as *infusions* or *tisanes,* are caffeine-free and may have medicinal properties as well. (A few are poisonous in quantity, so make sure you know what you're getting into when you try a new tea.) Many mix well with black tea, so it's worth experimenting with your own blends.

Now that you know all this, it's up to you to select a tea that you enjoy. If you like the smell of a tea, you'll probably like the taste.

Making and Serving Tea

Here's how to make a perfect pot of tea. It goes without saying that for excellent tea you should use loose tea, never a tea bag. If you hate the mess of loose tea, use an infusion ball (tea ball) to isolate the leaves.

Start with cold, fresh, good-tasting water—use bottled water if your tap water doesn't taste good. Bring the water to a boil and then pour a few ounces into the empty teapot. Cover the pot and swirl the water around for a minute or two. This will warm the pot. Toss out the water. Add the tea leaves—about 1 rounded teaspoon per cup of water. Pour in boiling water, put the lid on the pot, and let the tea steep for about 5 minutes before pouring.

"Shall I be mother?" is the wonderful English expression that means "Shall I pour?" A thin china teacup is the ideal vessel for the sacred fluid. Pour tea through a strainer. (It is a curious fact of life that pouring milk into the teacup before adding the tea makes much tastier tea than adding the milk to the tea.)

You can store tea in an opaque, airtight jar, in a cool, dark place for about a year.

Cocoa

Cacahuaquchtl is the Maya word for "the tree of the Gods." It refers to the cocoa tree, whose seeds were believed to be sacred. Mayas mixed the ground seeds with boiling water and then stirred it with twigs ("choc-choc" went the twigs against the side of their cups). Then they stirred in chile, ambergris, musk, or ground maize. Powerful stuff!

As part of the conversion of the ancient Mayas' descendants to Christianity, sixteenth-century nuns made their disciples dispense with the spices and add sugar and cream instead . . . heavenly!

Today, chocolatiers supervise the roasting of cocoa beans in jungle warehouses. Once roasted, the beans are broken and crushed to form the chocolate paste that will eventually be made into hot chocolate. Although cocoa beans are harvested in the third world, some of the finest chocolate is manufactured in Europe and the United States. Switzerland and the Netherlands are justly famous for their cocoa.

The best cocoa is not instant or "quick," and is certainly not made by adding boiling water. For a cup of excellent hot chocolate, put 1 tablespoon cocoa and 1 tablespoon sugar into a small saucepan. Add 2 tablespoons boiling water and stir to dissolve sugar and cocoa. Over low heat, add 1 cup milk. Continue stirring until all the ingredients are blended and the drink is heated through.

Cafe Amaretto

If you like the taste of almonds, you'll love this coffee.

MAKES ABOUT 2 CUPS.

2 heaping tablespoons ground coffee
1 cup water
1 cup milk

1 teaspoon almond extract
1 teaspoon sliced almonds

Prepare strong coffee according to your preferred method, using the ground coffee and water. Meanwhile, mix milk and almond extract and heat or steam. Pour coffee and milk into two mugs and garnish with almonds.

Variations

Try different flavorings, like orange extract or peppermint.

Hawaiian Coffee

Some of the best coffee in the world is Kona coffee, grown in Hawaii; here's a great way to prepare it. (If you can't find Hawaiian coffee, any strong coffee will work well with this recipe.)

MAKES 2 CUPS.

1 1/2 cups milk
2 tablespoons coconut syrup

2 shots espresso or 1/2 cup very strong
    Hawaiian coffee

In a small saucepan or with a milk steamer, heat the milk. Stir in the coconut syrup and the coffee.

Cinnamon Coffee

The perfect accompaniment to freshly baked muffins.

Makes 2 cups.

1/2 teaspoon ground cinnamon
1/4 teaspoon ground nutmeg
2 rounded tablespoons lightly roasted
   ground coffee

1 cup water
1 cup milk
1/2 teaspoon pure vanilla extract

Sprinkle cinnamon and nutmeg onto coffee grounds and then prepare with water according to your preferred method. Warm or steam the milk and stir in the vanilla. Pour warm or steamed milk into mugs and then pour in the coffee.

Indian Coffee

Imagine yourself in a far pavilion . . .

Makes 2 cups.

Pinch of ground cardamom
Pinch of ground ginger
2 rounded tablespoons dark roasted
   ground coffee

2 cups water

Sprinkle the cardamom and ginger onto the coffee grounds and then prepare with water according to your preferred method.

Arabian Mint Tea

An Arab friend served me this tea one morning and I spent the rest of the day on overdrive.

MAKES 2 CUPS.

2 cups water
4 teaspoons black tea leaves

1/4 cup fresh mint leaves
2 tablespoons honey

Bring 1 cup of the water to a boil and prepare strong black tea as described on pages 140–141. Meanwhile, simmer remaining 1 cup water with mint leaves and honey 5 minutes. Strain the mint tea into the black tea and serve.

Variation

Ginger Mint Tea

Add 2 slices ginger root to the mint before simmering.

Russian Tea

Strictly speaking, the way to drink Russian tea is to hold a sugar cube in your teeth while you sip hot tea prepared in a samovar. Here's another form of Russian tea, which your dentist will probably prefer.

MAKES 2 CUPS.

2 tablespoons blackberry or strawberry jelly
2 cups strong black tea, prepared according
   to the instructions on pages 140–141

2 lemon wedges

Place a tablespoon of strawberry jelly in each of two mugs or heatproof glasses. Pour on the tea and stir. Run the lemon wedge around the rim of the mug or glass; serve.

Strawberry Tea

The perfect drink for a spring morning.

MAKES 2 CUPS.

2 rounded teaspoons oolong tea leaves
2 cups boiling water

1/4 cup sliced strawberries

Prepare tea using tea and boiling water according to instructions on pages 140–141. Add strawberries and steep 5 minutes. Strain into cups and garnish with a few steeped strawberry slices.

Orange Tea

Here's a way to slip some vitamin C into your breakfast tea.

MAKES 2 CUPS.

2 whole cloves
1 cinnamon stick
1/4 teaspoon ground nutmeg
2 rounded teaspoons black tea leaves

1 cup boiling water
1 cup orange juice
1 tablespoon honey
2 thin orange slices

First, warm the teapot with boiling water, as described on pages 140–141. Toss out the water and add the cloves, cinnamon stick, nutmeg, and tea leaves. Pour in the boiling water and let tea steep 5 minutes.

Meanwhile warm the orange juice in a small saucepan over medium-low heat and stir in the honey. Remove the cinnamon stick from the teapot. Stir the hot orange juice into the tea.

To serve, pour the orange tea into cups through a strainer; garnish with orange slices.

Ginger Tea

Spice up your morning with this eye-opening variation.

MAKES ABOUT 2 CUPS.

About 10 thin ginger root slices
2 1/2 cups water

2 heaping teaspoons green tea leaves

Simmer ginger root and water in a small saucepan about 15 minutes. Warm teapot with boiling water as described on pages 140–141 and add tea leaves. Bring ginger-water to the boil and strain it into the teapot. Let steep 5 minutes and then serve.

Cozy Cocoa

This is the perfect rainy day treat.

MAKES 1 CUP.

1 tablespoon unsweetened cocoa powder
1 tablespoon sugar
1/2 teaspoon ground cinnamon
Dash of nutmeg

2 tablespoons boiling water
1 cup milk
1/4 teaspoon pure vanilla extract

Combine cocoa, sugar, cinnamon, and nutmeg in a small saucepan. Add boiling water and stir to dissolve cocoa and sugar. Place over low heat and stir in milk and vanilla. Heat, stirring, until hot.

Orangey Hot Chocolate

You won't have any trouble dragging your kids out of bed for this breakfast drink.

MAKES 2 CUPS.

2 tablespoons unsweetened cocoa powder
2 tablespoons sugar
2 tablespoons boiling water

2 cups milk
1/4 teaspoon orange extract
2 thin slices orange

Combine cocoa and sugar in a medium saucepan. Add boiling water and stir to dissolve cocoa and sugar. Place over low heat and stir in milk and orange extract. Heat, stirring, until hot.

Pour into mugs and garnish with orange slices.

Mexican Mocha

You'll feel like building your own temple to the gods of coffee and chocolate after just one sip.

MAKES 2 CUPS.

4 tablespoons unsweetened cocoa powder
4 tablespoons honey
2 tablespoons boiling water

1 1/3 cups milk
2 shots espresso coffee or 1/2 cup very
   strong coffee

Combine cocoa, honey, and boiling water in a small saucepan. Place over low heat and stir in milk. Heat, stirring, until hot. Stir in the coffee; serve.

Variation

For authentic Maya flavor, stir in a tiny dash of ground chile powder—*¡olé!*

Spiced Apple Punch

Here's a wholesome alternative to caffeinated drinks.

MAKES 2 CUPS.

2 cups apple juice
1 cinnamon stick
1 whole clove

Dash of ground ginger
Several very thin curls of orange peel

Combine apple juice with cinnamon stick, clove, and ginger in a medium saucepan and simmer over low heat about 5 minutes. Strain into mugs and garnish with orange peel.

Variations

Add a crushed cardamom pod and/or 1/2 teaspoon lemon juice and/or 1 teaspoon of minced crystallized ginger.

Cranberry Punch

Full of vitamin C and good for what ails you, this is another satisfying alternative to caffeinated drinks.

MAKES ABOUT 2 CUPS.

1 cup cranberry juice
1 cup apple juice
1/4 cup orange juice
4 whole cloves

1 cinnamon stick
Dash of ground ginger
2 thin orange slices
2 thin apple wedges

Combine juices and spices in a medium saucepan and simmer over low heat 10 to 15 minutes. Strain into mugs and garnish with orange and apple.

Hot Tomato Drink

You've got to try it to appreciate it.

MAKES 2 CUPS.

2 cups tomato juice
1 teaspoon fresh lemon juice
1 tablespoon finely chopped mint

Dash of hot pepper sauce (optional)
2 thin lemon slices

Combine all the ingredients except the lemon slices in a medium saucepan and heat over medium heat until hot. Pour into mugs and garnish with lemon slices.

Hot Lemonade

Here's another great way to add vitamin C to your diet.

MAKES 2 CUPS.

2 cups water
1 to 2 tablespoons sugar

2 tablespoons fresh lemon juice
2 thin lemon slices

In a medium saucepan, combine water and sugar and heat over medium heat until boiling. Remove from heat, stir in lemon juice and serve, garnished with lemon slices.

Sweet Treats

There are times—like when your Aunt Matilda is spending the night or your child is heading off to summer camp, or someone in the family needs cheering up or congratulating—when a bowl of muesli and a glass of skim milk just don't strike the right note. The recipes on the next few pages will help you through those times.

These are good breakfasts for weekends and special occasions—you can induce a real sense of being on vacation when you serve up, for example, Captain Dibbell House Breakfast Apple Pie or the Buttonwood Inn's To-Die-for French Toast. A number of these recipes came to me from bed and breakfast owners and innkeepers who know how to tempt the weekend guest.

You might serve these dishes for late breakfast or brunch—you can console your diet gods with the promise that you'll skip lunch and have a light dinner. Or plan on taking an all-day hike just as soon as the dishes are done. Another good act of contrition would be to serve plenty of fresh fruit and virtuous vegetarian side dishes with the heavier treats on offer here.

Captain Dibbell House Breakfast Apple Pie

Apple pie for breakfast? Totally decadent . . . and absolutely delicious. Be honest, haven't you ever sneaked a piece of last night's pie first thing in the morning? Make it official with this treat from the Captain Dibbell House in Clinton, Connecticut.

MAKES 4 SERVINGS.

Topping (see opposite)
1/2 cup packed light brown sugar
1 tablespoon cornstarch
3/4 teaspoon ground cinnamon
1 teaspoon apple pie spice
5 cups thinly sliced apples

Topping
3/4 cup all-purpose flour
1/4 cup packed light brown sugar
1/4 cup rolled oats
4 tablespoons butter, melted and cooled
   to warm

Preheat oven to 375F (190C). Spray a nonstick 2-quart casserole dish with nonstick cooking spray.

In a medium bowl, combine brown sugar, cornstarch, cinnamon, and apple pie spice. Add the apples and toss to coat apples. Layer the apple mixture into prepared casserole dish.

Make topping: In the same medium bowl, toss together flour, brown sugar, and oats. Stir in melted butter and mix gently with floured fingertips into moist crumbs. Sprinkle topping mixture over apples.

Bake 25 to 35 minutes or until the top is golden brown and the apples are fork tender.

Variations

About 5 minutes before removing from the oven, sprinkle pie with 1/2 cup grated Cheddar cheese. Or serve with a wedge of aged Cheddar.

Blanche's Honey Nut Rolls

From Blanche's B & B in Franconia, New Hampshire, these overnight rolls are a sweet, sticky treat. (No one will ever know you used frozen bread dough!)

MAKES 12 ROLLS.

1 loaf frozen bread dough, thawed
1/4 cup packed dark brown sugar
1/4 cup honey

1/2 teaspoon ground cinnamon
1/2 cup chopped walnuts or pecans
2 tablespoons butter, melted

On a lightly floured board, roll out the dough to an 18 × 12-inch rectangle. Sprinkle the brown sugar over the dough. Starting at one of the long sides, roll the dough up like a jelly roll. Slice crosswise into 1 1/2-inch pieces.

Spread the honey evenly over the bottom of a 9-inch nonstick pie plate. Sprinkle the cinnamon and nuts over the honey. Stand the dough pieces, evenly spaced, in the pie plate. Cover with a cloth towel and leave at room temperature overnight.

In the morning, preheat the oven to 325F (165C).

Brush the rolls with melted butter. Bake 25 minutes until lightly browned. Invert the pie plate onto a serving dish and serve hot.

Blackberry Cream-Cheese Coffeecake

This coffeecake from the Gosby House Inn, located in Pacific Grove, California, is rich and moist—a stunner for special occasions. I serve it topped with fresh mixed berries and a dollop of yogurt.

MAKES 6 TO 10 SERVINGS.

2 1/2 cups all-purpose flour
1 cup sugar
3/4 cup butter
1/2 teaspoon baking powder
1/2 teaspoon baking soda
1 cup sour cream

1 1/2 cups sliced almonds, toasted
  (see Note, page 22)
2 eggs
1 teaspoon almond extract
1 (8-ounce) package cream cheese, softened
1/2 cup blackberry preserves

Preheat the oven to 350F (175C). Grease and flour a 10-inch springform pan.

Combine the flour and 3/4 cup of the sugar in a medium bowl. Cut in the butter and mix until crumbly. (The easiest way to do this is to work the butter into the flour and sugar with your fingertips.) Set aside 3/4 cup of the mixture.

To the remaining crumb mixture, add baking powder, baking soda, sour cream, 1 cup of the almonds, 1 egg, and almond extract; blend well. Spread the batter over the bottom of prepared pan and about 2 inches up the sides of the pan. On the sides, the batter should be about 1/4 inch thick.

Beat the cream cheese, remaining 1/4 cup sugar, and remaining egg in a medium bowl, blending well. Pour over the batter in the pan. Carefully spoon the preserves over the cheese filling, to form a thin layer. Combine the reserved crumb mixture with the remaining 1/2 cup of almonds. Sprinkle this mixture over the preserves.

Bake 45 to 55 minutes or until the sides of the coffeecake begin to pull away from the springform pan. Let cool 15 minutes before removing the sides of the pan. Serve warm.

Variation

Any berry preserves will work, as will mixed berry preserves.

Black Friar Stuffed French Toast

Perry Risley, the innkeeper at the Black Friar Inn in Bar Harbor, Maine, sent me this recipe, which uses Maine products like maple syrup and blueberries. The sourdough bread offsets the sweetness of the maple syrup handsomely. He serves it with Black Friar Fruit Sauce on page 94.

MAKES 4 TO 6 SERVINGS.

6 slices sourdough bread, cut into
   1/4-inch cubes
4 ounces cream cheese, cubed
1 cup fresh or frozen blueberries
6 whole eggs

1/4 cup maple syrup
1 cup milk
1/2 teaspoon ground cinnamon
1/2 teaspoon ground nutmeg

The night before you plan to serve this dish, put half the cubed sourdough bread in a lightly greased 8-inch-square pan. Dot on the cream cheese, then add the fruit. Now cover with the remaining bread cubes.

In a medium bowl, combine the eggs, syrup, milk, and spices. Pour over the bread cubes. Cover with plastic wrap and refrigerate overnight.

In the morning, preheat the oven to 350F (175C). Unwrap the dish and bake 45 minutes or until set. Serve warm.

To-Die-for French Toast

With a name like that, it has to be great. This treat from the Buttonwood Inn on Mount Surprise in North Conway, New Hampshire, deserves its reputation. Innkeeper Peter Needham serves this French toast with his delicious spicy apple syrup (page 93).

MAKES 4 TO 6 SERVINGS.

1/4 cup butter or margarine
1/2 cup packed light brown sugar
1 tablespoon corn syrup
2 tart apples, peeled and sliced

1/2 loaf French bread, sliced
2 whole eggs
3/4 cup milk
1/2 teaspoon pure vanilla extract

The night before you plan to serve this dish, melt the butter in a small saucepan over medium-low heat.

Stir in the brown sugar and syrup and stir until blended. Spread this mixture onto the bottom of a 13 × 9-inch nonstick baking pan. Spread apple slices evenly over the sugar mixture. Arrange French bread slices over apple slices.

In a medium bowl, beat eggs until light and beat in milk and vanilla. Pour egg mixture evenly over bread. Cover with plastic wrap and refrigerate overnight.

In the morning, preheat the oven to 350F (175C). Unwrap the dish and bake about 40 minutes or until the bread is golden brown.

Anchor Watch Orange French Toast

Innkeeper Diane Campbell developed this dish for her husband, Captain Bob (of Balmy Day Cruises), and her guests at the Anchor Watch Inn in Boothbay Harbor, Maine.

MAKES 6 TO 8 SERVINGS.

1/4 cup butter or margarine	1 cup milk
1/4 cup honey	1 cup orange juice
8 slices bread (see Note below)	1 teaspoon grated orange peel
1 teaspoon ground cinnamon	8 orange twists (see page 16)
6 whole eggs	

Preheat oven to 350F (175C). In a small saucepan, melt the butter or margarine and pour into a 13 × 9-inch nonstick baking dish. Drizzle honey over the melted butter or margarine.

Arrange the bread in the pan, overlapping pieces to fit all the slices into a layer on the bottom of the pan. Sprinkle with cinnamon.

In a medium bowl, beat the eggs until light and beat in the milk, orange juice, and orange peel. Pour this mixture evenly over the bread. Cover with foil.

Bake 25 minutes, then remove the foil and bake another 5 minutes or until bread is puffed and lightly browned. Garnish with orange twists. Serve at once.

Note

This recipe works well with any kind of bread but Diane's favorite is a cinnamon swirl bread.

Orange Nut Bread

This yummy nut bread comes from the Governor's Inn in Ludlow, Vermont. Innkeepers Deedy and Charlie Marble slice the bread and make elegant little sandwiches using their Orange Cream-Cheese Spread (page 91). But the bread is certainly moist and flavorful enough to stand on its own.

MAKES 3 SMALL LOAVES.

2 cups sifted all-purpose flour
1 teaspoon baking powder
1/2 teaspoon salt
1/4 teaspoon baking soda
1/3 cup unsalted butter, at room
   temperature
1/2 cup sugar

2 eggs, beaten
1/2 cup fresh orange juice with pulp
1/2 cup water
1/2 teaspoon pure vanilla extract
1/2 teaspoon orange extract
1 cup chopped walnuts

Preheat oven to 350F (175C). Grease and flour 3 small (6 × 3 1/2-inch) loaf pans.

In a medium bowl, mix together flour, baking powder, salt, and baking soda.

In a large bowl, beat butter and sugar until creamy. Gradually beat in the eggs.

In a large measuring cup, combine orange juice, water, and extracts. Slowly add this mixture to the egg mixture, alternating with spoonfuls of the flour mixture until you have a smooth batter. Stir in walnuts.

Pour the batter into the prepared loaf pans. Bake 40 to 45 minutes or until a wooden pick inserted in the centers comes out clean. Cool in pan 10 minutes on a wire rack. Remove from the pan, cool completely and wrap. Chill well before slicing.

Blueberry Coffeecake

A beautiful coffeecake created at the Blue Lantern Inn located in Dana Point, California, this one is a classic. If you want a special treat, throw caution to the wind and serve with rum-flavored whipped cream.

MAKES 6 TO 8 SERVINGS.

Topping (see opposite)
2 cups all-purpose flour
2 teaspoons baking powder
1/4 cup unsalted butter, softened
1/4 cup sugar
1 whole egg
1/2 cup milk
1 pint (2 cups) fresh blueberries

Topping
1/4 cup unsalted butter, softened
1/4 cup packed brown sugar
1/4 cup all-purpose flour
1/2 teaspoon ground cinnamon
1/4 cup chopped pecans (optional)

Preheat the oven to 375F (190C). Grease an 8-inch springform pan.

Prepare topping: In a medium bowl, combine the butter, brown sugar, flour, cinnamon, and pecans, if using, with a fork to make a crumbly mixture. Set aside.

In a small bowl, sift together the flour and baking powder.

In a medium bowl, beat the butter and sugar until creamy. Add the egg and beat to combine. Add the flour mixture in 3 parts, alternating with the milk. Fold in the blueberries. Pour the batter into the prepared pan. Sprinkle topping mixture over the batter.

Bake 1 hour or until a wooden pick inserted in center comes out clean. Cool in pan on a wire rack. Run a knife around the edges and remove side of the pan.

Cappuccino Sorbet

Here's a special treat for the coffee lovers in your family.

MAKES 4 SERVINGS.

1 cup prepared espresso coffee, cooled
1 1/2 cups whole milk or half and half
1/4 cup sugar

4 cinnamon sticks
1 tablespoon unsweetened cocoa powder

Combine coffee, milk or half and half, and sugar in a medium bowl. Pour coffee mixture into an 8-inch-square metal baking dish or plastic storage container. Freeze 2 1/2 hours.

Remove the sorbet from the freezer, let it thaw slightly, about 10 minutes, then put chunks of sorbet into a blender. Process at high speed about 2 minutes, then return to the container and freeze overnight.

In the morning, take the sorbet out of the freezer and let it thaw slightly, about 10 minutes. Spoon sorbet into the blender and process about 1 minute or until frothy.

Pour the sorbet into 4 parfait glasses and garnish with cinnamon sticks and cocoa.

French Toast Fondue

Get out all your wedding gifts and go wild with this decadent dish.

Makes 4 servings.

Basic French Toast batter (page 84)
1/4 cup powdered sugar
Assorted syrups and toppings
   (pages 89 to 97)

6 slices bread
1/4 cup vegetable oil

First, spread the table with your best linens. Now set up your fondue pot in the center. Pour French toast batter into an elegant dish and arrange powdered sugar and toppings in your fine china bowls. Set the table with fondue forks at every place.

Use tiny, sharp metal cookie cutters to cut bread into bite-size shapes and pile the shapes into a napkin-lined basket. Assemble your guests at the table.

Pour the oil into the pot and heat until hot. The breakfasters should now skewer pieces of bread, dip them in the batter, cook them in the oil, dip them in the sugar and toppings and eat.

Note

Young children love fondue but the hot oil in this recipe makes it inappropriate for them. Supervise older children closely.

Setting the Scene

Imagine waking up in a four-poster bed at an elegant country inn. The smells of freshly brewed coffee and something fragrant in the oven come wafting up the stairs. Downstairs, classical music summons you to the breakfast room, where candles flicker in tiny bowls on a starched linen tablecloth. The table is set with fine china and sterling silver; a nosegay of flowers graces every setting. In short, a feast for the senses greets you before you even sit down to eat.

There's no reason you can't have the same sensory delight in your own home—if not every morning than at least some of the time. You probably spend more time creating a lovely atmosphere in the evening, especially if you have guests, than you do in the morning. But why not take the trouble to make breakfast special, too? Here are some ideas.

Be Prepared!

I've indicated elsewhere in the book ways of keeping morning preparation time to a minimum by mixing ingredients, setting the table, and loading the coffeepot the night before. The best intentions can easily be daunted when you're faced with making a meal from scratch first thing in the morning. So plan ahead.

Music

Classical music is soothing in the morning and new age music can be a gentle wake-up too. But if rock and roll is what gets your mojo working, go for it.

Place Settings

My friend Nancy believes strongly in certain place-setting niceties—a plate under the cereal bowl, for instance; milk in a pitcher, not straight from the carton—that make everyday breakfast a more civilized occasion. Another friend, Anne, uses lots of dishes to disguise the fact that she's serving less at breakfast than she used to: a side dish for toast, a saucer under the juice glass, and so on gives the illusion of a big spread. Of course all of this can create more dirty dishes than you're willing to wash in the morning, but that shouldn't stop you from using a nice set of matched china. If you're feeling extravagant in the china department one day, pick up a special set of breakfast dishes—something bright and cheery for the morning. If you're serving hot food, consider warming the plates. (You can warm them by putting them in the oven at a very low temperature while you cook breakfast. Or put them in the dishwasher, on the dry cycle.)

Linens

If you're into tablecloths, consider setting a double cloth before you go to bed. Spread the evening's solid color damask on the bottom and then cover with a slightly smaller, floral cloth for breakfast. After breakfast, whisk off the floral cloth and you're ready for the next meal. Cheery napkin rings can carry you through the day or can be replaced by more formal evening rings.

Take It Outdoors

If you have an outdoor eating place, don't wait for a barbecue to use it! In pleasant weather, watching the dew dry and listening to the early birds chirp can be an excellent start to the day. You'll probably get fewer bugs at this time of day, too. Fill a wicker basket with your cutlery, napkins, and serving utensils before you go to bed. A thermal tea or coffeepot saves trips back inside for more.

Pack a Picnic Basket

Probably the perfect way to start the day is with a brisk hike. If there are two of you, fill one backpack with a Thermos® of hot drinks and a batch of warm muffins wrapped in foil and stored securely in a plastic container. In another backpack, carry a plastic container full of fresh fruit mixed with yogurt and an icy collection of fruit juices.

Breakfast in Bed

Instead of facing the great outdoors, snuggle in for a luscious breakfast in bed. A few words of advice: Pancakes are excellent breakfast-in-bed choices, as are French toast and waffles. Consider one of the oven-baked French-toast dishes on pages 87 and 155–157, so the whole family can enjoy the breakfast, too. Use a large tray, preferably one with legs that fit over the lucky person's legs. You might place a small table near the breakfaster for extra space. Line the tray with an unfolded cloth napkin and set with your best china.

A single flower in a bud vase is lovely but liable to topple over. Transfer it to the nearby table or instead tuck a single stem into a folded napkin or use edible flowers to garnish the main dish.

If you have a CD or tape player in the bedroom, put on some soothing music but avoid the jarring sounds of the radio. On the other hand, the breakfaster may appreciate the morning paper. If you are a child making breakfast in bed for a parent, remember that the best part of having breakfast in bed is being allowed to sleep late beforehand. This will make almost any food you give your parent taste heavenly. If you are serving your parent cereal, take a tip from one youngster who learned the hard way and *don't* pour the milk on half an hour before you serve the breakfast. If you're planning to breakfast *a deux,* do plenty of advance planning the night before so that you can assemble the food quickly and snuggle back into bed before the rosy glow of nighttime is gone.

Dog's Breakfast

A "dog's breakfast" is a happy combination of leftovers pulled from the refrigerator at the last minute. I've seen people enjoy a reheated slice of pizza or a bowl of couscous salad in the morning. One friend finished off the bowl of tiramisu I'd brought to her dinner party the night before. There's no reason not to eat foods for breakfast that are usually consumed later in the day. Your child might enjoy a peanut butter and jelly sandwich first thing in the morning, whereas you may want to heat up last night's egg drop soup.

Second Breakfast

When Hans Castorp, the hero of *The Magic Mountain,* comes down to breakfast at the sanitarium where his cousin is receiving treatments, the table is laid with "pots of marmalade and honey, basins of rice and oatmeal porridge, dishes of cold meat and scrambled eggs; a plenitude of butter, a Gruyère cheese dripping moisture under a glass bell. A bowl of fresh and dried fruits stood in the centre of the table." *And that's only first breakfast.* A few hours later, he's back for second breakfast, where the same feast has been laid again, along with pitchers of fresh milk. (Hans opts for a beer instead of the milk.) You may not want to go this far, but there's much to be said for having a little food to tide you over first thing in the morning—a slice of toast or a piece of fruit—and then a larger meal mid-morning. Especially if you have houseguests, it's pleasant to have juice, coffee, and a basket of rolls or bowl of fruit available from the time you get up and then offer a full, sit-down breakfast around 11:00 A.M., when everyone is up and about.

Breakfast Buffet

A welcome sight to visitors who are spending the night at your home is a breakfast buffet that lets them select the kind of foods they prefer in the morning. A cold selection of cereals, fresh fruit salad, yogurts, and milk might stand beside a basket of warm muffins. Add a platter of oven-baked French toast and your meal is complete. Set up your coffeepot in the dining room and make it clear that guests are welcome to help themselves. Tea drinkers might select from a basket of herbal and regular teas.

Appendix

Addresses of Inns

If you aren't in the mood to cook, you may want to sample the fare at one of the inns mentioned in this book. Here are the names and addresses of the inns which contributed recipes to *The Creative Breakfast*:

Anchor Watch Inn
P.O. Box 535
Boothbay Harbor, ME 04538
(207) 633-7565

Black Friar Inn
10 Summer St.
Bar Harbor, ME 04609
(800) 753-0494

Blanche's B & B
351 Easton Valley Road
Franconia, NH 03580
(603) 823-9550

Blue Lantern Inn
c/o Four Sisters Inns
P.O. Box 3073
Monterey, CA 93942
(408) 649-0908

The Buttonwood Inn on Mount Surprise
P.O. Box 1817
North Conway, NH 03860
(800) 421-1785

Captain Dibbell House Bed and Breakfast
21 Commerce St.
Clinton, CT 06413
(203) 669-1646

Edgecombe-Coles House
HCR 60, Box 3010
Camden, ME 04843
(207) 236-2336

Gosby House Inn
c/o Four Sisters Inns
P.O. Box 3073
Monterey, CA 93942
(408) 649-0908

The Governor's Inn
86 Main St.
Ludlow, VT 05149
(800)-GOVERNOR

Hidden Meadow Bed and Breakfast
40 Blood Street
Lyme, CT 06371
(860) 434-8360

High Meadows Vineyard & Mountain
    Sunset
High Meadows Lane
Scottsville, VA 24590
(804) 286-2218

Hillcrest Guest House
Box 4459
Rutland, VT 05701
(802) 775-1670

L'Auberge Provençale
P.O. Box 119
White Post, VA 22663
(800) 638-1702

The Maples Inn
16 Roberts Avenue
Bar Harbor, ME 04609
(207) 288-3443

Molly Stark Inn
1067 East Main St.
Bennington, VT 05201
(800) 356-3076

The Inn at Round Barn Farm
RR 1, Box 247
Waitsfield, VT 05673
(802) 496-2276

1024 Washington Bed and Breakfast
1024 Washington St.
Bath, ME 04530
(207) 443-5202

Windermere Manor Bed and Breakfast
P.O. Box 2177
Lake Arrowhead, CA 92352
(909) 336-3292

Metric Conversion Charts

Comparison to Metric Measure

When You Know	Symbol	Multiply By	To Find	Symbol
teaspoons	tsp.	5.0	milliliters	ml
tablespoons	tbsp.	15.0	milliliters	ml
fluid ounces	fl. oz.	30.0	milliliters	ml
cups	c	0.24	liters	l
pints	pt.	0.47	liters	l
quarts	qt.	0.95	liters	l
ounces	oz.	28.0	grams	g
pounds	lb.	0.45	kilograms	kg
Fahrenheit	F	5/9 (after subtracting 32)	Celsius	C

Fahrenheit to Celsius

F	C
200–205	95
220–225	105
245–250	120
275	135
300–305	150
325–330	165
345–350	175
370–375	190
400–405	205
425–430	220
445–450	230
470–475	245
500	260

Liquid Measure to Liters

1/4	cup	=	0.06	liters
1/2	cup	=	0.12	liters
3/4	cup	=	0.18	liters
1	cup	=	0.24	liters
1-1/4	cups	=	0.30	liters
1-1/2	cups	=	0.36	liters
2	cups	=	0.48	liters
2-1/2	cups	=	0.60	liters
3	cups	=	0.72	liters
3-1/2	cups	=	0.84	liters
4	cups	=	0.96	liters
4-1/2	cups	=	1.08	liters
5	cups	=	1.20	liters
5-1/2	cups	=	1.32	liters

Liquid Measure to Milliliters

1/4	teaspoon	=	1.25	milliliters
1/2	teaspoon	=	2.50	milliliters
3/4	teaspoon	=	3.75	milliliters
1	teaspoon	=	5.00	milliliters
1-1/4	teaspoons	=	6.25	milliliters
1-1/2	teaspoons	=	7.50	milliliters
1-3/4	teaspoons	=	8.75	milliliters
2	teaspoons	=	10.0	milliliters
1	tablespoon	=	15.0	milliliters
2	tablespoons	=	30.0	milliliters

Index

About the Author

Ellen Klavan has written for *Woman's Day, Parents, Working Mother, American Baby* and other magazines. She is the author of four books, including *The Creative Lunch Box*. She is married to the author Andrew Klavan and has two children.